Other Books by Aaron Hass, Ph.D.

Teenage Sexuality: A Survey of Teenage Sexual Behavior
Love, Sex, and the Single Man
In the Shadow of the Holocaust: The Second Generation

The Gift of Fatherhood

How Men's Lives Are Transformed
by Their Children

Aaron Hass, Ph.D.

A FIRESIDE BOOK
Published by Simon & Schuster
New York   London   Toronto   Sydney   Tokyo   Singapore

F

FIRESIDE
Rockefeller Center
1230 Avenue of the Americas
New York, New York 10020

"Cat's in the Cradle" on page 7

© 1974 Story Songs, LTD. Used by permission.

Designed by Marysarah Quinn

Manufactured in the United States of America

2   4   6   8   10   9   7   5   3

Library of Congress Cataloging-in-Publication Data

Hass, Aaron.
The gift of fatherhood : how men's lives are transformed by their
children / Aaron Hass.
p.   cm.
"A Fireside book."
1. Fatherhood.   2. Father and child.   I. Title.
HQ756.H38   1994
306.874'2—dc20   94-6410
                                                    CIP

ISBN: 0-671-87582-5

For Rebecca, the love of my life

Acknowledgments

My thanks to Marilyn Abraham for believing in the project and for her ongoing encouragement of my writing. Ed Walters was a superb editor. His recommendations significantly enhanced the manuscript. My copy editor, Red Wassenich, was meticulous. Thank you Bob Bishop and JoAnn Uno for your help on the computer. My wife, Rebecca, as always, was my reader of first resort. Her instincts are invariably right on the mark. Finally, I extend my gratitude to Richard Pine for coming up with a great title.

CONTENTS

My child arrived just the other day.
He came to the world in the usual way.
But there were planes to catch and bills to pay
He learned to walk while I was away.
And he was talkin' fore I knew it.
And as he grew he'd say,
"I'm gonna be like you, Dad.
You know I'm gonna be like you."

And the cat's in the cradle and the silver spoon,
Little boy blue and the man in the moon.
"When you comin' home, Dad?"
"I don't know when, but we'll get together then, Son.
You know we'll have a good time then."

My son turned ten just the other day.
He said, "Thanks for the ball, Dad. Come on, let's play.
Can you teach me to throw?"
I said, "Not today. I got a lot to do."
He said, "That's okay."
And he walked away, but his smile never dimmed.
It said, "I'm gonna be like him, yeah.
You know I'm gonna be like him."

And the cat's in the cradle and the silver spoon,
Little boy blue and the man in the moon.
"When you comin' home, Dad?"
"I don't know when, but we'll get together then, Son.
You know we'll have a good time then."

Well, he came from college just the other day,
So much like a man I just had to say,
"Son, I'm proud of you. Can you sit for a while?"
He shook his head and he said with a smile,
"What I'd really like, Dad, is to borrow the car keys.
See you later. Can I have them please?"

I've long since retired, my son's moved away.
I called him up just the other day.
I said, "I'd like to see you if you don't mind."
He said, "I'd love to, Dad, if I can find the time.
You see, my job's a hassle and the kids have the flu,
But it's sure nice talkin' to you, Dad.
It's been sure nice talkin' to you."

And as I hung up the phone it occurred to me,
He'd grown up just like me.
My boy was just like me.

"Cat's in the Cradle"
Words and Music by Harry Chapin and Sandy Chapin

PROLOGUE

Despite all the developmental theories I had digested, despite my extensive training as a clinical psychologist, despite all the patients I had seen over the years, I was unprepared for what fatherhood really meant until I had my own children.

I was unprepared for the overwhelming feelings of love and protectiveness I would feel toward my children.

I was unprepared for the energy my children would require of me.

I was unprepared for the ambivalence I would feel about their presence.

I was unprepared for the ongoing demands they would make upon me.

I was unprepared for the ensuing, continuous struggle to find a balance in my life.

I was unprepared for how the importance of my family would change my life perspective forever.

I was unprepared for how much pleasure my children would give me.

I was unprepared for how anxious and frightened I would feel about them.

I was unprepared for the profound changes which would take place in my marriage after my children were born.

I was unprepared for the awesome opportunity and responsibility to shape confident, happy human beings I had acquired.

I know that I am not the only father with these sentiments. But no one really prepared me for the considerable changes and feelings which fatherhood brought, and I would guess that no one has prepared you either. The most important role of our lives, and we have been left to navigate on our own.

The adjustments required of fatherhood have not been easy ones for me. I was single until I was thirty-five and, therefore, lived a fairly carefree life, with few ongoing responsibilities to anyone. For the most part, I did exactly as I wanted, whenever I wanted. Getting married and, particularly, having children changed all of that. And I still struggle with the consequences of those changes.

I wrote this book in order to help you articulate the many feelings which may have accompanied the presence of your children. I also wanted to provide you with some helpful skills and guidelines so that you can have the most satisfying relationship possible with your sons and daughters. I wrote this book in order to reassure you that fathering is a continuous process which has its inevitable ups and downs. You will falter and you will soar.

I am not always as patient with my children as I should be. I do not always understand my children well enough. I do not always leave my personal frustrations at the door so that I can be the dad my children need. I do not always completely focus on my children when I am playing with them. I do not spend as much time with my children as I should. I do not always enjoy my children as much as I could.

But I'm getting there.

And so can you.

INTRODUCTION

This is not a book about extremely dysfunctional families. Nor is it a book about fathers who are abusive toward their children. It is a book about you and me, fathers who have the best of intentions, fathers who want to have closer relationships with their children. Some of us don't know how to relate to our children. Some of us know what we should do but find it difficult to follow through effectively. Some of us, because of our personalities or individual frustrations, find ourselves without the necessary patience required for parenting.

The Gift of Fatherhood will first help you understand the forces which have kept you from becoming a more involved dad. It will then provide clear, simple steps which will enable you to enjoy your children more, be more loving and patient with them, and perform the trying task of effectively disciplining them. And hopefully, it will help you understand the rewards of fatherhood while you're still able to enjoy them.

Six feet tall, suntanned, trim, and dressed in his double-breasted blue blazer, fifty-eight-year-old Mark Brian* looked the epitome of the very successful entertainment attorney. His clients appeared on the covers of national magazines, and his telephone calls to the titans of his industry were immediately accepted. He was a major player, and his name struck a chord of admiration and envy among his colleagues. To his credit, Mark's status was initially achieved by seventy-hour work weeks and not by inherited connections. His father was an immigrant who toiled seven days a week in his candy store, which was located in a lower middle class neighborhood of Brooklyn.

Mark had come to see me because of nagging doubts and an ill-defined sense of emptiness. Thirty minutes into our first session, I asked him, "What do you regret most in your life?" His eyes immediately watered. I had clearly struck an exposed nerve ending. "That I didn't spend more time with my kids. . . . When they were growing up, I was never home. We never had a relationship . . . and now it's too late." A tear streamed down his right cheek.

As we age, most of us accumulate regrets. Not having spent enough time with my children, not having expressed more feelings toward my children, not having a certain closeness with my children are laments often verbalized by fathers whom I encounter. Yet, if you ask most young fathers, "What is most important to you?" they will answer, "My children" or "My family." Unfortunately, their articulated priority is often not reflected in how they live their lives, most particularly, in how they apportion their time and where they direct their energies.

"Would you play with me, daddy?"

"After I finish watching the game."
"After I read the newspaper."
"I promise I will on the weekend."
"I'm tired right now."
"I've got some important work I have to do."
"This is not a good time."
"I'd like to, but . . ."

---

* For reasons of confidentiality, pseudonyms have been used throughout the book.

It is easy for you to justify not spending more time with your children. "I have to work long hours so that I can provide for them," you righteously argue. "I have to work long hours so I can give them everything I didn't have," you sadly tell me. Indeed, we live in difficult economic times. However, upon closer scrutiny, it is often apparent that these statements are rationalizations, a means to avoid an arena from which you do not derive a great deal of pleasure or self-esteem.

Men feel good about themselves because of what they achieve. Men derive a sense of satisfaction from the status they attain. That's how we measure ourselves, that's how we determine our success. You don't get recognized by your peers for being a good father. You engender their respect because of how much money you make, how much power you yield, how productive you have been. And we are always comparing. Is his bigger than mine?

You work long hours during the week. You arrive home tired, harried, stressed out. You have little patience for your children. What you want most is peace and quiet. You spend fifteen minutes of "quality time" with them before they go to sleep, but you are distracted and not all there. On the weekend, you want to relax, catch up on some reading, watch a ball game, play some golf. By all accounts, you deserve this respite after another tough week. You resent any more demands being placed on you. "When do I get some time just for me?" you plead.

Becoming a better father requires an examination and reconsideration of the forces which have shaped our male ideal. In order for you to want to be a better father, you must see fathering as important for you and for your child. Indeed, you must perceive fathering as a noble endeavor, one which enhances your humanity and uniquely enriches the lives of your sons and daughters whom you cherish so dearly.

How successful have you been as a father and as a person?

Do you always keep your promises to your child?

Does your child know how much you love him/her?

How often do you do something with your child that you find completely boring?

How effective are you at getting your child to be open with you about his/her problems?

How do you react when your child says, "I hate you"?

Your children need you. They need your love, your support, your encouragement, your protection. *And you need your children, as well.* You need them to give you perspective about what is really important in life. You need their love. You also need them so you can become a more loving, giving, patient, and positive person.

Being the human creatures we are, these observations will only seem like intellectual objectives at best, and platitudes at worst, unless you learn to truly enjoy the process of fathering, instead of approaching it as one more responsibility or chore. I will help you derive more pleasure from your relationship with your child. You don't have to be a psychologist to understand the necessity of positive reinforcement in encouraging new behavior. For that is my goal—to have you change the way you relate to your children.

Many men are at least unconsciously ambivalent about having children. Yes, of course, I'll probably have children, he acknowledges. But the keen desire, the intense urge is often lacking. Children mean responsibilities, lifelong responsibilities. Children will divert my energies from what's really important to me—my work. Children will interfere with my marriage. Children will require me to give more of myself, to lose more of myself.

I tell men that having children is potentially psychologically healthy for them. Good fathering implies a willingness to give up some of our self-centeredness. Good fathering requires the defeat of some of our overbearing narcissism. When you are being a good father you are loving another unselfishly, without ulterior motive. And when you are a good father, you will reap the rewards of love and closeness which will more than compensate for what you fear you may lose. You will feel less driven to achieve, less driven to impress. You will feel more relaxed and more at peace with yourself.

If you are a better father, you will have a better marriage. If you are a better father, you will have a better sex life. (You will have to wait until Chapter Eight for an explanation of that one.) If you are a better father, your values will shift from the materialistic to the interpersonal. You will care more about people and less about tangible or material measures of success. You will feel freer. If you are a better father, you will become more sensitive to the feelings of others as well as your own. If you are a better father, you will be able to teach good values to your children because you will be demonstrating them by your own behavior.

Jonathan Mann is a thirty-four-year-old chemist. He has been married for eight years and has a son, Andrew, who is seven, and a four-year-old daughter, Elisa. "I've never felt comfortable with children," Jonathan told me. "When I was a child, I was pretty much a loner. I've always felt more comfortable with books than with people. At least with adults, I can have an intellectual conversation. I'm not at all athletic. I can't play baseball or shoot baskets with my son. I have no idea what to do with my daughter. She's into Barbie dolls and changing clothes five times a day. What do I have in common with her?"

The awkwardness Jonathan feels with his children is not unusual. But it can be overcome. You will need to find common ground with your children. You can learn how to relate to them, how to speak with them, how to be with them. First, you must learn the necessary skills, then you will practice, and then you will feel more comfortable, more natural.

When my first child, Rachel, was born, I remember how clumsy and inept I felt even just holding her. I learned how to change a diaper, but I remember saying to my wife, "I can't change a diaper with poop, only with pee." That convenience lasted exactly two hours. The next time Rachel pooped, my wife took me by her side at the changing table and demonstrated the wiping procedure. From then on, I was expected to change any kind of diaper. And I did.

When we haven't learned something and we tell ourselves "I can't do that," we often feel awkward and reluctant to try it.

Once you have the experience and practice the procedure, you will be surprised at how comfortable you can become. You will think back to the old, incompetent feeling you had and shake your head in disbelief.

Chris Strong, a thirty-seven year old insurance salesman, won three letters as a high school athlete. Chris was overjoyed on the days of the births of his two sons. He wanted boys. He could do what he enjoyed most with them—play ball. He could teach them. He could experience his own youth all over again.

No matter what the sport—football, baseball, or basketball—Peter, his older son, was enthusiastic and a quick study. He was competitive. He had that fire. He imbibed the passion which his father transmitted. However, Chris's younger son, Steve, was a disappointment to his father. "Steve is introverted, studious, and completely uninterested in athletics," Chris remarked. "I feel bad about it, but we just haven't been able to connect."

Steve was uninterested in what his father enjoyed most in the world. Unfortunately, his father, therefore, became uninterested in him. Shaking his head, Chris explained, "We just don't speak the same language." All fathers have hopes and dreams for their children. How do we cope with the inevitable disappointments because our children do not simply mirror those hopes and dreams? How do we stay focused on our child's needs and proclivities and hold our own needs at bay? How do we encourage our children to fulfill their potential, instead of trying to steer them in the directions we hope they will take? How can you connect with your children even though they seem so different from you?

A further word about Chris and his older son, Peter. While Chris and Peter did a lot of things together, it became apparent that their relationship was not a close one. Although it came as a surprise to him, Chris eventually acknowledged that he didn't really know Peter. He didn't know that sixteen year old Peter was very shy and uncomfortable around girls. He didn't know that, while Peter received decent grades, he, nonetheless, felt academically inadequate, particularly when he compared himself to his brother, who always seemed to receive straight A's. Chris didn't know that Peter drank too much. Yet, for all these years, Chris had accepted the illusion of closeness, the illusion of knowing his child. Peter was an athlete like he had been. From this all-important symmetry, Chris made all too many misguided assumptions of who Peter really was.

"They will only listen to their mother," Alan Karlin, a thirty-three year old father of two daughters complained to me. "And they only want to be with their mother," he continued. Why might that be so? Why do children indicate a clear or even overwhelming preference for one parent? Is it simply the gender similarity between child and parent? Or is it perhaps more—the manner in which the parent relates to the child, the sincere interest the parent demonstrates in what the child does or says, the greater patience the parent evidences, particularly when the child is at his/her brattiest, or the greater empathy the parent communicates to the child. Nurturing behavior may come more naturally to women than men, but men can learn to be as nurturing as their spouses. And when men become better at relating to their children, they will enjoy it more, which will make them want to do it more, and a self-reinforcing cycle will have begun.

Alan's children "only listen to their mother." Why is it so difficult for Alan to discipline his daughters? Why does he seem to spend so much time in the role of disciplinarian when he is interacting with his daughters? Could the answer to this last question have something to do with why Alan's children "only want to be with their mother"?

Being a better father must include an understanding of the direct and indirect effects which the ups and downs of your marriage have on your children. Most of us are not conscious of how we displace our resentment from our mate to our children. How many times have you snapped at your daughter when you were really angry with your wife? A family is a dynamic unit. Changes or upheavals in one part of that unit always impact the other parts. Therefore, we must also understand how difficulties with our children may affect our marriage. Finally, it is crucial that you understand how your feelings about your wife and your marriage affect your desire to parent. And, ultimately, the more involved you are with your children, the more appreciative, more loving, and more devoted your wife will be with you.

Living in the 1990s, so many men must cope with the complexities of being a single, divorced dad, or a divorced dad in a blended family with stepchildren and/or children from the new marriage. The testing of allegiances, the inordinate need for reassurance (on the part of both the child and the parent), the intricate web of jealousies, the uncertain boundaries, all make the task of fathering more difficult. But these obstacles can be overcome if they are first understood and openly acknowledged.

Obviously, you are reading this book because you feel that something is missing from your role as a father. You would like to do better—both for yourself and for your children's sake. Beginnings are difficult, but let's start.

Next Sunday, take your child for ice cream. Just you and your child. (If you have more than one child, take each of them on successive Sundays, or earlier, if you can manage.) Sit down in the ice cream shop and talk with your child. Maintain eye contact. Ask him/her about his/her friends, his/her favorite activities. Tell your child some things about you, about your life, about your childhood. Don't be in a hurry. Indicate that this is what you want to be doing now, more than anything else in the world.

Back at home, before you walk in the door, give your child a hug. Allow the hug to linger a few seconds. Release the embrace and look your child in the eye. Now, say it. "I love you. I love you very much."

CHAPTER ONE

The Twelve Obstacles to Fathering
(and How to Overcome Them)

Make a commitment.

I will be the father I would have liked to have had.

The wisdom you have gained through years of experience allows you to evaluate your own childhood. Think about what you missed in your relationship with your father. Do some of the following come to mind?

I wish he had spent more time with me.

I wish he had talked more with me.

I wish he had asked more about my feelings.

I wish he had told me he loved me.

I wish he had been more interested in me.

I wish he had hugged me.

I wish he had encouraged me more.

I wish he had been more supportive of what I wanted to do and become, rather than pushing me in the direction that he wanted for me.

I wish he had been happier when he was with me.

What else would you add to your particular wish list? Write

it down. It will help you focus on the important roles you can play in your children's lives.

_____

_____

_____

_____

_____

_____

_____

_____

Having a child may evoke previously repressed feelings of anger, frustration, deprivation, and resentment toward your own father. (Having a child also makes us appreciate how difficult it is to be a parent.) Those unconscious hurts may drive you away from your children or they may propel you toward them as you attempt to give your children what you never received. ("I'll never do that to my child when I'm a parent," you swore to yourself many years ago. Alas, how difficult we find it not to repeat the patterns which were inflicted upon us.) In either case, you need to be as aware as possible of the influences of the past on your present circumstances.

No one sits us down and teaches us about parenting. No one gives us a course as we go through school. However, girls, at least, are continually reinforced for acting in a nurturing, empathic manner. They often learn more than boys about parenting because of their identification with their mothers as role models.

Most boys grow up with no analogous opportunity. Your father was probably someone who left in the morning, came home in the evening, financially provided for his family, and spent relatively little time actually interacting with his children. He was not someone to whom you turned on a daily basis for help, advice, or reassurance. That wasn't his job, you assumed.

Even as adults, we find women's magazines filled with articles about parenting. You won't find any such articles in magazines which cater to men. Parenting is not part of my responsibility, you therefore continue to assume. It has nothing to do with being a man. It is irrelevant to being a success, you believe.

A few men were lucky enough to have had terrific dads. He played with you. He talked with you. He took you on special outings with him. He put his arm around your shoulder when you walked together. But most of us did not grow up with an *involved* father. Most of us did not grow up with an *engaged* father. For, unfortunately, your father was trapped in the role model which his father provided. We, in turn, often mimic our fathers' approaches.

The results of a survey published in the September 1991 issue of *Harper's* magazine reflect these attitudes. While thirty-one percent of Fortune 1000 companies offer paternity leave, only one percent of eligible men have taken advantage of it. Many men may not believe they can afford to take time off. But surely, more than one percent could weather the temporary financial deprivation, even if it were only for a brief period of time. Clearly, men want to go to work for powerful reasons having little to do with money.

Social barriers die hard, but institutional barriers to active fathering are gradually coming down. Thanks to the Family and Medical Leave Act of 1993, parents who work at companies which employ more than fifty persons can take up to twelve weeks of unpaid leave to allow them to care for newborns. Undoubtedly, many mothers will take advantage of this dispensation. It remains to be seen how many men will do the same.

Companies should encourage men to take a more active role in parenting. The reality, however, is that many consider taking leave to be tantamount to "career suicide." People at the top should set an example. However, *Redbook* (June 1993) reported that when Catalyst, a New York City–based employment/research group asked personnel directors and CEOs how much paternity leave would be reasonable, sixty-three percent said "none."

For most men, work comprises the greatest part of their identity. Ask a man who has been laid off from his job how he feels. You will probably hear, "I feel like I'm not worth anything anymore." The workplace is where men have derived their self-esteem.

But the reality is that today you have greater freedom than ever to choose how involved a parent you will be. You are neither bound by traditional cultural expectations nor doomed to repeat the patterns laid down by your own father. *You can redefine what fathering will mean for you.* You can make fathering an important, stimulating, rewarding, and significant part of your ongoing life.

Twelve Reasons Why You Might Not Want to Spend More Time with Your Children

Parenting Is Difficult

Almost all parents will tell you that child rearing is much more difficult than they had anticipated. Before your first child's arrival, your fantasies involved playing with him or observing him proudly. The scenes were always pleasant, always gratifying. You did not anticipate colic, tantrums, "I hate you," defiance, disappointment, or purple hair.

While it is true that "the years fly by," when you are going through a taxing developmental period of your child's life, time can move very slowly. Whether it is the sleep deprivation and resulting crankiness you experience during your child's infancy or the anxiety you feel during your child's adolescent forms of rebellion, fathering is stressful as well as joyful. By the time your child leaves home forever, you will have made thousands of decisions affecting his or her life, and you will have agonized about whether those decisions were the right ones. Fathering does not occur naturally or easily. But you can learn to be more patient, more giving, more loving, more generous, and more forgiving than you ever thought you would be.

You Wait Too Long Before Becoming Involved

You should bond with your child even before he comes through his mother's birth canal. It can begin when you first put your hand or your ear to your wife's bulging abdomen, when you participate in childbirth classes, or when you view the ultrasound image of the fetus. Unfortunately, many men view infancy as a time of closeness between mother and child. They may not want to "interfere." Many men also feel terribly awkward handling a baby or involving themselves in the baby's natural functions. ("I don't change diapers!" or "I change diapers, but not if the baby has diarrhea!") You may believe that you can't feed her as well, dress her as well, burp her as well, or understand her cries as well as your wife can. Oftentimes, men do not view their children as fun until they can play and become involved in activities which the father enjoys.

The relative lack of early contact with your child has a circular effect. The older your child becomes without a bond having been established, the more awkward you and your child will feel when you are together. And the more awkward you feel together, the less you will want to engage each other again.

The more time you spend with your child, the more you will enjoy that time. You and your child will build familiarity, a closeness. In addition, you won't have to deal with your child's resentment because of the lack of time you have devoted to him. When a father infrequently plays with his child, the child's resentment over his feelings of deprivation hamper the quality of the encounter. He is angry and impatient with you, which causes you to feel impatient and alienated from him, which causes him to feel even more deprived and angry with you, and so on and so on. This is one of the reasons fathers are so disappointed when, after having failed to spend time with their children for protracted periods of time, they plan a special day together and it bombs. You may come with the best of intentions, full of enthusiasm and energy. But your child greets you with old hurts.

Don't postpone your fatherhood.

You Made an Attempt to Engage Your Child and You Were Rebuffed

You approach your child and say, "Let's play together," or, even better, you say, "Let's play whatever you would like." Your child says, "No thanks, dad. I don't want to play now."

You feel rejected. ("Well, if he doesn't want to play with me, to heck with him.") You feel hurt and self-righteous about not offering again. "I tried," you say to yourself.

But certainly you would agree that, just because *you* found the time to play with your child at that particular moment, it is unreasonable to assume that your child will necessarily want to interrupt what he may be involved with in order to respond to your unexpected overture. He may also be reluctant to accept your offer for fear of being disappointed once again because your interest will not last very long.

Don't let your ego interfere.

Instead of walking away and shaking your head after your child says, "Not now, dad," simply respond with "Okay, let's make a specific date for another time. What do you think might be fun? When would you like to do it?"

You See Your Child as a Burden Rather Than a Joy

Oftentimes, fathers view play with their children as another thing they have to do. They already feel tired and overwhelmed by other obligations and worries. Perhaps they are unable to effectively compartmentalize their lives. They are unable to leave their work at the office. They are unable to prevent their marital frustrations from spilling over into their relationships with their children. They are unable to cease obsessing about their financial straits. Or they may simply see themselves as inadequate, awkward fathers and wish to avoid the anxiety associated with this perceived deficiency.

The more competent you feel as a parent, the more joy you will derive from fathering. Obviously, the less "baggage," the fewer burdens you bring to your fathering, the freer you will be to spontaneously and enthusiastically play with your child. Fathering can provide an arena for personal growth. When you are actively fathering, you will develop aptitudes and sensitivities which will serve you well in the myriad of other roles you play in your world.

Your Children Seem to Have Arrived from Another Planet

The music they listen to, the clothes they wear, the language your children speak may all seem alien to you. You have forgotten how wide a gulf *you* perceived there to be between you and your father when you were a child. You can't relate to any of it, so you don't take an interest in any of it. *And so you imagine a much wider gap between you and your child than actually exists.* Your child may act differently, talk differently, dance differently, or eat differently than you did when you were his age. But he has the same *emotional* needs that you had. He needs your affirmation, your understanding, your love. He needs a close relationship with his father.

You Feel More Comfortable with Your Son Than Your Daughter

It begins early, even before the birth. Fathers usually wish to have a boy. Research indicates that fathers touch their infant sons more than their infant daughters. Throughout the child's formative years, fathers spend more time with their sons than their daughters. Those fathers who have a very strong masculine identity, who perhaps are very athletic, demonstrate a clear preference for spending time with their sons than their daughters. Those fathers who fervently hope that their sons will follow in their footsteps as physicians, lawyers, businessmen, will also stay close in order to plant and fertilize those seeds. On the other hand, those fathers who also identify themselves with their sensitive, emotional side will more likely feel comfortable with daughters than men who adhere to rather rigid stereotypes about how a male should behave. *Having a closer relationship with your daughter will facilitate the development of your interpersonal sensitivities and emotionally empathic capacities.* Your daughter can push you to more fully realize all aspects of your self.

The Temperaments of You and Your Child Don't Seem to Fit

"My son is so different from me. Is he really mine?" you wonder aloud. "What do I have in common with my little girl?" you plead. Fathers are often confronted with children whose interests seem to be completely different from their own. Athletically inclined fathers are terribly disappointed when they face sons who perhaps prefer music, art, or computers to the rough and tumble, competitive world of sports.

But you can always find a way to relate to him. Even if there is no seeming "common ground," take this opportunity to expand your own horizons and diminish your feelings of estrangement from your child. You must move into his spheres of interest. Your child will be happy to share his activity with you if he perceives you to be genuinely interested. Having a different temperament from your child provides you with a challenge and an opening. The stage will be set for you to "stretch" your self-concept, to experience parts of yourself which you previously had dismissed or never even discovered.

You Have a Very Difficult Child

Difficult children are difficult to be with. Instead of pleasure, they often provide stress and frustration. Instead of offering joy, they cause you to wish you had a different child. You find yourself being *continuously* critical of him. You believe that he can't do anything right. It is natural to want to withdraw from interactions which are painful and unrewarding.

Before I had my own children, I believed that our socializing environment was predominantly responsible for who we become. Particularly after having my second daughter, who from day one was so temperamentally different from my first daughter, I began to fully appreciate the predominant influence of our unique, genetic blueprint. There is no getting around it. No matter how effective, consistent, or patient a parent you may be, some children will prove more problematic, more troublesome, more stressful to be with, more volatile in their moods—in short, more difficult, or to put it in a positive light, more challenging than others.

Ironically, it is the more difficult child who needs you the most. He hears your constant criticisms. He sees your looks of exasperation. And he feels terrible that you think those things about him, for he is desperate for your love. He is desperate for you to tell him he is not the bad person who he suspects everyone (including himself) believes him to be. He needs your encouragement. He needs you to believe in him. He needs you to go the extra mile. He needs you not to give up on him. He needs you to love him no matter what.

How do you not lose patience with a difficult child? By relating to his insecurities. Your child is so bossy because inside she feels so powerless. Your child is a brat because inside he feels frightened and out of control. Your child does exactly what you just told him was not permitted because he feels worthless and anticipates your rejection. Your child doesn't allow himself to hear your words of praise because he feels so unlovable.

"But, I've given him my love and attention," you insist.

"Why does he still feel so insecure?" Remember, your child was *born* with a propensity to develop in particular temperamental ways. His insecurities, therefore, may be an ongoing part of his life. But you can ease his burden. You can keep his insecurities from destroying him.

There is no one in the world who has more power and potential influence to help your child feel better about himself than you. And there is no one in the world who can better teach you how to be more patient and self-sacrificing than your own difficult child. The patience, self-control, and generosity you can learn from raising a difficult child will also help you better deal with the most problematic, most troublesome people you will inevitably encounter in your lifetime.

You Feel Financial Pressures

After the arrival of your child, your sense of overwhelming responsibility as a father and as a provider really kicks in. Some men almost feel a sense of panic and want to run away. To make matters worse, perhaps your wife stopped working or drastically cut back her hours. Even though you may want her to be home with your new baby, her lack of financial contribution increases the load you feel. Ironically, just as you should be diverting some of your attention to your newborn, you feel the pressure to work longer hours in order to give your family what you want them to have. Furthermore, as your children get older and reach an age when they may need you the most, you are moving through your thirties and forties, your "professional prime," a time when you feel you must give your career all of your efforts in order to obtain a certain level of status and security.

The more children you have, the more justified you may feel in not devoting more time to them. You feel even more financial pressure. You work even longer hours. You're tired and you say to yourself, "I work hard all week. I've already fulfilled my responsibilities to my family—and then some." And you infer, "I've already demonstrated how much I care about my family."

Oftentimes it is difficult to distinguish your drive to succeed in your career from the realistic financial obligations you must meet. It is more socially acceptable to invoke the latter than former in justifying your absence from family life. It appears less selfish to blame your financial responsibilities than to acknowledge your more narcissistic strivings for success when you work on weekends or arrive home after your child's bedtime.

Your children need you. They need your attention, your encouragement, your wisdom, your physical contact, your affirmation of how important they are to you. They need your love more than they need a CD player or a $100 pair of sneakers. And you need to be with your children so that you can develop a healthier perspective and balance in life.

You Believe Parenting Is Your Wife's Responsibility

You may believe that parenting comes more naturally to your wife than to yourself. *She's got the maternal instinct. Mothers raise children. That's what my mother did. Women just know what to do with children, how to be with them,* you believe. And so you rationalize your relative lack of involvement with your children by subconsciously saying to yourself, They're better off with her anyway.

Furthermore, many men believe that parenting is mostly the female's responsibility. If you accept this notion, then you may not feel completely comfortable being an actively involved father because you will have entered a feminine domain. Fathering might actually detract from your sense of masculinity. Until you incorporate nurturing and attachment to your children into your male ideal, you will feel that attention to these aspects of life will actually weaken you. Have you noticed that when most men get together in order to bond and affirm their manliness, they speak about four topics—sports, money, work, and sex? Children are what women talk about, you assume. Unfortunately, the quality of your relationship with your child does not garner you the esteem of your peers. Will you be strong enough, secure enough as a man, to fly in the face of convention?

Your Children Prefer to Be with Their Mother

Perhaps you have asked your child, "Would you rather go with mom or dad?" You felt rejected when she said, "I want to go with mom." They prefer to be with their mother, you tell yourself.

It may indeed be the case that your child would rather spend time with your wife than with you. But perhaps that's because your wife is more enthusiastic, more appreciative, or more attentive than you are when interacting with your child. While most daughters (particularly younger ones) might gravitate toward their mother, it is not unusual to find a girl who chooses to be with her father because he is more fun to be with, because he makes her feel so special, or because he indicates by his demeanor that he truly enjoys and looks forward to his time with her.

Your daughter may, in fact, appreciate the differentness of being with a man, her dad. The relationship which each parent has with their child is unique. As a father, your role need not be to imitate your wife's behavior when you are interacting with your daughter. On the contrary, you can provide your daughter with another flavor of positive role model which will help her establish later relationships with a greater variety of people. She will also have two different styles or approaches to life to draw upon when making future decisions.

Children want to be with a parent who clearly demonstrates his/her love, interest, and enthusiasm while being with them. You will feel the satisfaction of being wanted and loved when your children feel that too.

You Avoid Being with Your Child to Avoid Marital Conflict

Couples often disagree about how to raise their children. You may perceive your wife to be too indulgent, too lax. She may, just as firmly, believe you to be unrealistically demanding or too stern with your son or daughter. You may believe she coddles your children, spoils them. Your wife, because of past feelings of deprivation, may see in you the father who withheld his love from her when she was a child. Old resentments may be displaced onto you if she perceives you to be repeating the same pattern with your children.

So you leave the field to her in order to avoid another argument. And you rationalize your withdrawal from childrearing by saying to yourself that you want to keep a somewhat shaky marriage from becoming even more unsatisfying and, perhaps, ultimately untenable.

If the prospect of marital conflict interferes with your desire to be with your children, you must resolve that conflict, instead of withdrawing from family life. Begin by talking with your wife about the kinds of parenting which each of you received. How did you feel in your relationships with your parents? What were your perceptions of your parents as you were growing up? How did your relationships with your parents affect your subsequent romantic relationships and the kinds of partners you chose? Successfully defusing the tension between you and your wife may require some professional assistance in unraveling old childhood hurts which affect the way each of you now approaches your children and your mate.

Ultimately, of course, the development of better communication skills in your marriage and greater empathy for one another will serve you in good stead in developing a more communicative and empathic relationship with your children.

All husbands and wives who I see in my practice have had both their marriage and their parenting styles affected by the mother and father who reared them. In their own ways, Ben and Barbara reflect many of the issues which I have discussed in this chapter.

Ben, a thirty-eight year old accountant, and Barbara, a thirty-six year old teacher, had been married for seven years before they appeared at my office because of marital difficulties which had been simmering for years. (No one seeks psychotherapy or counseling after experiencing a problem for only a short period of time.) There were the usual complaints. From Ben: Barbara didn't seem to have much time for him anymore. Barbara was overly involved with the children. Barbara had put on weight and didn't care about her appearance. Barbara wasn't interested in sex. From Barbara: Ben was uninvolved in family life. Ben seemed to care more about his work than about her or the children. Ben always excused himself as being too stressed or too tired. Ben wasn't affectionate anymore. Ben didn't seem to care about having an emotionally close relationship anymore.

Both Ben and Barbara grew up in very modest circumstances. Their parents occupied traditional roles. Ben's father worked seven days a week as a tailor in Boston. Barbara's father worked overtime in his steel mill whenever it was available. Ben's mother and Barbara's mother were housewives. Ben's father, an immigrant, was from "the old school." "Be happy for what you have," "Life is tough," "You don't need very much," "Money doesn't grow on trees," were some of the lessons he imparted to Ben. Barbara's father, abandoned by his parents at an early age, was a bitter, cold man. He was uninterested in his children. Barbara remembers her frustration at repeatedly attempting to gain his attention or a word of approval. He virtually ignored Barbara and her brothers.

Ben learned his lessons well. Both as a child and as an adult, Ben has led a life of self-denial. Although his financial circumstances are significantly different from his father's, unfortunately Ben feels as though and acts as though he is living under the same constraints. And he expects the same of his children. "My children always seem to be whining or complaining about this or that. And their mother spoils them rotten. What kind of character will they grow up with? Shouldn't there be limits?" Ben rhetorically asked.

Barbara was more aware of her previous hurt and anger toward her father than Ben was of his feelings of deprivation. She was determined to provide for her children what she never received. She admitted, "It's difficult for me not to give my children what they want. But, unlike Ben, I don't see my children as being so demanding or unreasonable." And Barbara acknowledged that, in many ways, particularly when there is an issue of giving, she sees her father when she observes her husband. Every time Ben says "No" to his children (or to her), Barbara hears that voice from her childhood denying her once again.

In any couple I see in therapy, both parties are absolutely convinced of the correctness of their point of view. Each is dumbfounded that the other doesn't see "the obvious." But the issue, of course, is not who is right or who is acting most appropriately. In Ben and Barbara's case, one of the first steps in their treatment was for them to understand how the parenting which they received has affected their feelings and expectations toward their own children. Only then can they respond most helpfully to the needs of their children, as opposed to acting on the sanctions of their own childhood.

Why You Should Want to Spend More Time with Your Children

You Will Understand Their Abilities Better

The more time you spend with your children, the more attuned you will be to their emerging abilities. Those fathers who spend little time with their children frequently either underestimate or overestimate the developmental progress of their sons and daughters. If you underestimate your child's competence, you won't provide adequate challenge or stimulation. Your child will be bored. If you overestimate your child's skills, your unrealistic expectations will prove to be a frustrating and unpleasant experience for him and you. In either case, your child will be less motivated to interact with you in the future.

The more time you spend with your children, the more realistically you will be able to assess their capacities and the more aware you will be of their particular talents and sensibilities. You will, therefore, have the optimal opportunity to provide challenging and stimulating interactions. You will discover not only what they enjoy doing, but how they enjoy doing it. (For example, adult rules may be inappropriate when playing a game with a six-year-old. There are probably one hundred different ways you can play a game with a basketball.)

And, don't forget to let your children win, at least some of the time. No one enjoys playing something at which they always lose.

You Will Enhance Your Child's Self-Esteem

Your time is precious to both you and your child. Your willingness to give your time to him sends a message: You are important. A father who gives of himself implicitly communicates his love and respect for his child. And if you, the person your child respects most in the world, believe he is worthy of your undivided attention, your child will bask in the sense of his own importance.

Perhaps I need not mention the obvious: There is nothing more valuable for our psychological well-being than healthy self-esteem. You can help provide that for your child. And when your child grows up, you will relish the pride you feel and savor the knowledge that you had a hand in cultivating the person she has become.

You May Be Able to Forestall Childhood Problems

As parents, we do not have as much control as we would like over our children's lives. We wish our children were more popular. We wish our children were less awkward. It pains us to see them hurt, rejected by their peers. We wish we could protect them from all of that. But we can't.

However, the closer the relationship we have with our children, the greater our opportunity to provide them with self-respect and self-acceptance. Less involved fathers may facilitate the opposite reactions. For example, in a recent article published in *American Psychologist,* Dr. Louise Silverstein writes: "Research clearly documents the direct correlation between father absence and higher rates of aggressive behavior in sons, sexually precocious behavior in daughters, and more rigid sex stereotypes in children of both sexes."

You Will Have More Influence on Them

Your child is exposed to many influences. And the older he becomes, the more he is likely to adopt his peer group's frame of reference. But the closer the relationship you have with your child, the more likely your child will continue to identify with you. You will, therefore, be in an advantageous position to instill your positive values and increase the likelihood that they will be accepted. The more love and respect (as opposed to fear and anger) your child has for you, the more likely it is that he will incorporate his sense of you in himself. He will act more like you.

It is to be expected that your son will be more likely to identify with and feel closer to you than your daughter may. However, you will still be a terribly important role model for her if she feels a loving connection between the two of you. And she will be more likely to choose a man who will reflect your positive traits for her lifemate later on.

It Will Enhance Your Self-Esteem

The more time you spend with your baby or your five-year-old, the better at fathering you will be. Given the fact that fathering does not come naturally and must, instead, be learned, you will gain a sense of self-satisfaction as you become more accomplished at it.

In the case of your relationship with your children, the old adage, "The more you put into it, the more you'll get out of it," readily applies. For as you sense how increasingly important your child feels you to be, you, in turn, will feel an increasing sense of self-importance.

Because of Your Epitaph

Your children will be gone soon.

As your children reach later and later developmental stages, you will look back with amazement and wistfulness at how quickly it went, how quickly your sons' and daughters' innocence and childlike dependence on you evaporated. "Where was I when they were growing up?" fathers ask themselves. "Why didn't I realize then, how important they were to me?"

Unfortunately, for many men, looking back upon their lives does not produce satisfying reflections. Questions such as, "What did I do with my life? Did I attend to what was really important?" are met with aggrieved answers. When asking, "What did I accomplish?" oftentimes we find our replies to be hollow. When you reach that stage of life when you are prone to evaluate the choices you made, I want your answer to be a much more satisfying one.

You Can Do It Right

If you approach fathering as one more task, one more job, you almost guarantee that it will not be an enjoyable one. If you appreciate the benefits which you and your child can derive from your interactions, you will act with enthusiasm and expectation. Your eagerness will infect your child, and you will both know that the other cares, that the other loves.

The more your children separate from you, the more they will be shaped by their peers and by their own culture. We increasingly fret over their well-being as they slip away from our protective shield. But we can lay a foundation which will enable them to make the right choices. We can insure that they feel loved, so they do not reach out for recognition in destructive ways. And when they are conflicted and cannot make up their mind, we can create a relationship which invites discussion and is open to guidance.

You cannot undo your childhood. You can never receive what you deserved from your own father. But you are in the fortunate position of seeing to it that your child has the parent he is entitled to have. You have been given the chance to do it differently, to do it better, to do it right.

Make a list of what you resolve to do more of with your child. If you need some ideas to get started, return to the list you made at the beginning of this chapter.

_____

_____

_____

_____

_____

_____

_____

_____

_____

Our tendency is to imitate what we have seen in our own fathers and to cast our expectations after those. *Don't repeat the mistakes which your father made.* Being a better father to your children can help heal the disappointments of your own childhood. As your life becomes more gratifying, as it becomes filled with love, you will find that your longtime, gnawing resentments toward your father will recede. You won't need to be angry any longer because your life will feel fulfilled.

Don't waste time blaming yourself for what you have or have not done with your children to this point. It is understandable that, to the extent you have not built a closer relationship with your child, you will feel more alienated and, perhaps, helpless now. The good news is that it is not too late.

Your responsibility as a parent is to nurture your child, to help him reach his fullest potential. *Your child also presents you with an opportunity to grow.* Seize that opening.

CHAPTER TWO

Learning to Love Your Child More

First, a brief assessment. Answer true or false to the following statements:

I hug my child a lot.

I frequently tell my child, "I love you."

I am successful at getting my child to open up to me about his problems.

When my child says, "I hate you," I don't simply react. Instead, I try to understand why he is so angry.

When my child talks to me, I stop what I'm doing and listen to him.

I give my child a lot more praise than criticism.

I am patient with my child.

I am able to control the frustrations in other parts of my life and not take them out on my child.

I am able to effectively set reasonable limits for my child.

I show my child I respect him.

I help my child verbalize his feelings.

I am conscious of telling my child what I like about him.

How many statements received an unequivocal "True"? If your score was fifty percent or more, you are doing well. Soon, you will be doing even better. If you responded "True" to far fewer than fifty percent of the statements, you will be amazed at the transformation which will occur in your relationship with your child as your score improves.

Does Your Child Feel Loved?

Just because you love your child does not mean that he feels loved. You must demonstrate your love. Your *actions* and *comments* will allow your child to know that he is loved, that he is valued by you. All too often, during a session in my office, I have heard a father say in front of his child, "But, he knows I love him." And I have seen his son shake his head in disbelief and reply, "You sure don't *act* that way."

Demonstrating love for your children does not imply giving them everything they want. Children need limits. Children want limits. They need to know that someone is looking out for their welfare because they doubt their own ability to do so, and rightly so. Children fear their impulses and want their parents to keep them from getting in over their heads.

Many fathers shower their children with *things*. But children often sense that you are buying their love. They mistrust you because you are giving them toys or jewelry or clothes instead of giving yourself. We are often unaware of what we are doing since we tend to fall into the same trap of buying ourselves something in order to make ourselves feel better. So you purchase a trinket for your sons or daughters to make them feel good about themselves and about you. But after a while, it simply does not work for your child, as he becomes increasingly aware that his hunger for love, his hunger for you, has not been satiated. And even if your gifts superficially satisfy your child's emotional cravings, he will later confuse being loving with giving things.

Too many fathers have had the following experience after

coming home from an out-of-town business trip. Your child hears you open the front door and rushes at you. "Daddy, what did you bring me?" Not, "Daddy, I missed you," or "Daddy, I'm so happy you're back," but, "Daddy, what did you bring me this time?"

Some fathers fake caring in other ways. Your child runs up excitedly and says, "Daddy, I want to show you something." He proceeds to take you into his room where he reveals the science project he completed that day at school. While he launches into a detailed explanation of the project, you look interested and even nod your head in acknowledgment several times. You act as though you are engrossed, but you're not. You don't ask any questions. You don't comment. You don't show any enthusiasm. You're not involved. And your child will soon sense your detachment. *Children are extremely adept at perceiving phony interest and counterfeit caring.*

Developing Empathy Toward Your Child

One of the most important ways to show that you care, one of the most important ways you can demonstrate your love, is to value what your child values. You must indicate that because he is important, what is significant to him is significant to you. And what will enable you to actually feel that excitement is your ability to put yourself in your child's shoes. You must see the world through his eyes. You must feel the experience as your eight-year-old feels the experience. Your ability to mirror the enthusiasm of your child will depend on your ability to try on his perspective. Observe your child's pride at his Lego creation, her self-satisfaction at the "beautiful tree" she has just drawn. Share their marvel.

Of course, this process is not just vital for participating in pleasurable experiences with your child. Your child is crying because he made a critical error during the baseball game. Your child is upset because her friend failed to invite her to the sleep-over party. You want to make him/her feel better. You have the best of intentions. You say, "Don't get upset. It's not worth it."

However, when you say, "It's not worth it," what you are really saying is that it would not be worth it to you. But at that moment, it is upsetting to your child because it is vital to him. You must place yourself in her frame of reference. You need not agree with your child that his feelings are appropriate. But you must understand why he would feel that way and acknowledge (instead of avoiding) his feelings. "I know it must be embarrassing to have dropped that ball. I understand you probably feel terrible for letting your team down." "I know you feel rejected because Sally didn't invite you to her party." If you want your child to feel that he is loved, that he is important to you, then he must know that what is important to him is also important to you.

It is easier to feel empathy for a peer because you share the same frame of reference. Experiencing empathy for your child requires more effort. You must appreciate his youthful vulnerabilities, his lack of perspective, the urgency of his desires, his difficulty tolerating frustration, and the seeming life-and-death drama of his everyday world. The reason your child does not react to events as you do (or as you would like him to) is simple. He is not an adult.

Think about how hurt, rejected, and unimportant you felt when you were saying something which was important to you to someone who was significant to you (i.e., someone from whom you seek validation) and it was clear that he was not listening, was distracted, or wished you would finish quickly so he could move on.

Now imagine how you might have felt when you were five and your father or mother did that to you.

Without meaning to, many fathers find themselves on the wrong side of this kind of situation.

"Dad, I want to tell you about the field trip we took at school today."

"I can read the newspaper and listen to you at the same time."

Maybe you *can* listen to your child and read the newspaper at the same time. *But your child won't feel as though you are listening.* When you listen attentively to your child, you will imbue him with a sense of self-worth. When your head is buried in the newspaper, when you do not make eye contact with your child while he is speaking to you, he will feel as though what he has to say, what his life is about, is unimportant.

It is not enough to listen to your child. You must *show him* that you are listening. If your child does not perceive you to be listening, your attention will have lost its potential impact.

It is also not enough for you to understand what your child is saying. You must *demonstrate* that you understand by translating your understanding into words. If you say to your child, "I understand how you feel," he may still believe, "No, you don't." After all, your child may think, "You're not me," "You don't really know me," "You haven't proven you understood me in the past."

Most men are not very comfortable with their feelings. To feel is to allow yourself to be vulnerable, men believe. "Being tough" implicitly means suppressing your feelings. ("What's the point of crying?" my father used to tell me. "Just fix it," or "Just do it better next time," he urged.) Fathers want their children (especially their boys) to be strong, so they often discourage them from expressing their emotions.

Everyone wants to feel understood by others. Everyone wants their feelings to be respected. Sometimes, in their efforts to help their child "fix it" or "do it better," fathers inadvertently give the impression that they don't understand and that they don't value and respect their child's feelings.

"Oh, it's not so bad," or "You shouldn't feel that way," or "That's not a good reason to get upset."

Not only do your children's feelings make you uncomfortable, but your instinct is to protect your son or daughter, to spare them emotional harm. However, your denial ironically produces additional distress. For now, your child feels neither understood nor validated. And because he feels misunderstood and, therefore, hurt by you, he withdraws, experiencing more alienation now than before.

Before you ask questions, before you offer reassurance, before you volunteer advice, before you launch into a minilecture, try to empathize with your child's feelings. You want to communicate (1) that his feelings are important (both to you and to him), (2) that you understand those feelings, and, hence, (3) that you understand him.

For example, what's missing from each of these fathers' responses?

"Marjorie doesn't want to be my best friend anymore," your daughter cries.

"Don't worry, honey, you'll make another best friend," you reply.

"I just know I'm not going to do well on that test tomorrow," your son frets.

"You'll do great," you reassure him.

"You spend more time with my sister than with me," your older child protests.

"Your sister is going through a difficult time and needs me a lot these days," you explain.

"You never give me anything!" your child complains.

"Don't say never! It's not true and it's not fair. If you want something, you can just ask me politely for it," you answer.

"I can't get Billy to ever want to play with me," your child laments.

"Why don't you find out what his favorite game is and then invite him over to play it," you advise.

"Mom won't let me sleep over at my friend's house, but she lets sister do it," your child complains.

"Why do you think she lets your sister and not you do that?" you inquire.

In each of these examples, the father's well-meaning response doesn't show the child that he values or understands the child's feelings.

One of the best ways to do this is to employ a device we call "reflection." While reflecting your child's feelings, it is as if you are holding up a mirror to his subjective experience and putting that experience into words.

"Marjorie doesn't want to be my best friend anymore."
Instead of "Don't worry, honey, you'll make another best friend," try "That must hurt a lot."

"I just know I'm not going to do well on that test tomorrow."
Instead of "You'll do great," try "I know you're nervous because it's so important to you."

"You spend more time with my sister than with me."
Instead of "Your sister is going through a difficult time and needs me a lot these days," try "I understand that you're feeling neglected by me."

"You never give me anything!"
Instead of "Don't say never! It's not true and it's not fair. If you want something, you can just ask me politely for it," try "I'm sorry you feel that I don't love you."

"I can't get Billy to ever want to play with me."
Instead of "Why don't you find out what his favorite game is and then invite him over to play it," try "I know you're feeling frustrated and probably rejected too."

"Mom won't let me sleep over at my friend's house, but she lets sister do it."

Instead of "Why do you think she lets sister and not you do that?" try "I can see why you would feel angry because it seems so unfair."

By using reflection, you give your child's feelings a name and you enable your child to articulate them more clearly.

"I hate Emily because she wants to be with Lisa now more than she wants to be with me," your daughter screams.

"You sound angry. You're feeling hurt that maybe Emily doesn't want to be your best friend anymore," you reply. And, then, you might validate your daughter's feelings. "It would hurt me too if my best friend did that to me."

After you reflect your child's feelings, she will probably elaborate because she will sense that you care and that you understand her. After she is finished, you can then provide advice, reassurance, or an opportunity to explore the dilemma further. Reflection is a powerful tool that you can utilize in any relationship in which you want to engender a feeling in the other of being cared about and being understood.

Responding empathically is not something which occurs naturally. It takes practice to effectively demonstrate your understanding and undivided attention. Students in the mental health professions may spend years mastering the skillful use of reflection. If you are preoccupied or emotionally unavailable and do not respond empathically when your child approaches you, you can return to him at a later time in order to indicate that you care. "I was thinking about what you said before and . . ." Your conscious efforts will be greatly appreciated, for you will have reassured your child that you did hear him and that you did understand ("Gosh, he really was listening and he even thought about it.") And because your child will not be feeling as distressed at this later time, your empathy may have even more of an impact.

Empathy requires that you put yourself in the other's frame of reference. Remember that in order to empathize with your child, you must see the world and experience the world through his immature capacities. Your child seems to use the words "never," "always," or "completely" so frequently because of his relative inability to tolerate frustration, his lack of patience, and his undeveloped perspective. You must understand the immediacy of your child's world in order to fully appreciate his feelings.

"I hate my brother, Sam," your child informs you.

"No, you don't," you reply.

But at that moment, your older son does hate his baby brother. He hates Sam because Sam takes away some of your love and attention from him. If you were your son, you would probably feel exactly the same way toward Sam. So why do you get so upset when your child uses such forceful words as "hate"? Because on a reactive level, you fear that this might be a permanent state of affairs. But we all sometimes hate those we love. Remember, then, that these feelings of hatred are transitory. They, too, will pass.

Your ongoing compassion and empathy for your child's emotions will likely lead to an increase in empathy for your spouse, your parents, your co-workers, and anyone else with whom you have ongoing contact. Instead of simply reacting, you will begin to reflexively ask yourself the question: Why did he act that way? What feelings are behind that behavior? You will like yourself more when you operate in this manner, and others will appreciate your consideration of their feelings (a consideration which hardly anyone else ever gives them).

If you teach your child the value of empathy by your behavior, your child will be more likely to practice this skill with you and his peers. You will be creating a more empathic, sympathetic human being. Think about your own father. You probably believe, "He never really understood me. He never knew who I really was." You can provide the understanding which your child longs for.

Keeping Criticism Under Control

I have painfully observed many fathers who are *continuously* critical of their children. It appears as though criticism is their only currency of communication. Not surprisingly, these fathers experienced childhoods of harsh judgments and cruel evaluations from their own parents. When I point out their exacting, oppressive style of relating to their children, these fathers first protest that my characterization is too one-sided. "I'm not *always* critical," they reply. But when I present this type of father with the incontrovertible evidence (such as a tape of the interaction between him and his child), he often falls back on, "Well, *I* turned out okay, so if it was good enough for me. . . ." But the fact of the matter is that it wasn't "good enough for him." For this father turned out to be an angry, self-critical man who often feels that he is not in control and must, therefore, punish his child as a means of asserting control.

"Why can't you do it the *right* way?" this father yells at his child. What he means, of course, is, Why can't you do it the way an adult would do it? But children do not do things the way adults do them *because they are children.*

Many fathers need to consciously work at interrupting their reflexive, steady stream of criticism. All of us who want to be more verbally loving with our children need to make the effort. While our personal frustrations may produce a response such as, "No, I can't play with you. Can't you see I'm busy!" our desire to be more generous mandates a more loving reply: "I'm busy now but I'll be finished in one hour. Can we play then?" Relating in this more considerate manner can become habitual as well.

People who are highly critical of others are also apt to set unrealistic standards for themselves. In order for a father like this to become less critical of his child, he must become less exacting, kinder, and more forgiving toward himself. If you are overly disparaging of your son, he, in turn, will judge himself harshly. He will learn to doubt himself and expect his failure.

Criticism of your child will engender a negative self-image. It may also create the dynamic of a self-fulfilling prophecy. If your child hears, "Can't you do anything right?" or "You'll never amount to anything," you will not only undermine her confidence, but you will probably sap her motivation to try. Think back to who was critical of you while you were growing up. Did that criticism have a long-lasting impact of self-doubt and self-deprecation?

Before you misread me, let me assure you that I am being neither naive nor pollyannaish. I know your child is not perfect. I know that your child does not always behave as he should. But being honest with your child need not imply that you must tell him, "You're just not cut out for that," when instead, you could say, "I'm proud of you for trying." If you think, "He'll never _____" or say to him "You'll never _____," how can you be sure of that in any case? Fortunately, my files are filled with letters from parents who were former patients which begin, "I never would have believed that my child would ever. . . ."

Dr. Hass may be correct, you admit, about most kids, but my child never does *anything* right! you insist. But I will wager that your child does hundreds of things right—she is creative in the way she dresses (even though you can't stand these new styles), she is generous with her friends (even though you think she gives too much of herself), she is inquisitive (even though she exasperates you with her endless questions), she is able to become absorbed in her reading (even though it maddens you that you have to repeatedly call her to the dinner table).

It is best to completely avoid the word "never" when evaluating your child's behavior. There are four potential consequences of using that word, all of them detrimental. (1) Your child protests, "But what about when I. . . ." Now you are in a battle about whether or not "that counts" or whether "that was the same thing." As you debate this issue, you move away from the circumstance at hand. (2) You create a sense of resignation in your child as he says to himself, What's the point of trying if I'll never get it right. (3) Your child not only defeats himself, but he also distances himself from you by believing, What's the point of ever doing it right if I never get recognized for it. (4) Because of his anger, your child makes matters even worse as a means of goading you further. "I'll show him what a *really* messy room looks like," or "He thought that was a bad report card? Wait until he sees the next one."

There is no greater gift you can give your child than self-esteem. I have often had the following sad experience in my office. A father who is highly critical of his child finishes recounting the list of grievances. "Johnny can't do _____." "Johnny won't do _____." "Johnny doesn't ever do _____." "Johnny is always _____." He pauses and then, in an off-handed way, remarks, "But, basically, Johnny is a pretty good kid." And when I press him further to tell me what Johnny does right, he can, indeed, enumerate a different kind of record. Unfortunately, this father rarely comments to his son about what he is doing well. And consequently, his son rarely feels good about himself. *Let your child know what is right about him.*

Your child needs your *encouragement* to be the best she can be. Remember the teacher, the coach, the relative who assured you, who believed in your abilities? If you were fortunate enough to have had such a person in your life, you are also probably aware of the profound consequences of that early inspiration. Too many parents do not give their children enough credit or recognition for what they *can* do. Unfortunately, as a result, these children do not give themselves enough credit either.

You need not be lavish with your praise, but don't be stingy either.

The more specific you can be, the more effective your compliments will prove. So instead of simply, "That was great!" you might say, "It took a lot of courage to. . . ." Or instead of, "That was wonderful!" you might say, "That was really creative the way you were able to. . . ." By being specific in this manner, you are not only reinforcing the lessons your child has learned, but you are facilitating the incorporation of those labels (courageous, creative) into his self-image.

Dr. Haim Ginott, the noted child psychologist, points out a potential danger in praising a child's character as opposed to his efforts and/or accomplishments. When a child does not feel as though he is as completely "wonderful" as you say, such as when he is aware of harboring contrary impulses or fantasies, he will feel anxious because he will believe he is being misunderstood or that he has fooled you. He may then even act in a way which purposefully contradicts the label you have just bestowed upon him, just to set the record straight.

Tell your child what you like about him. Recognize his achievements. If your child's room is tidy, you probably don't remark about it because that is the way you assume it should be. But most children's natural tendency is to mess up their rooms. Keeping them neat requires effort. Recognize it!

"Well, does that mean that I should simply ignore it when my child screws up?" you may wonder. When your child drips chocolate ice cream on the couch or crashes into an expensive vase or knocks over the pitcher of milk at breakfast, he already feels clumsy, embarrassed, and terrible about himself. Why should you feel compelled to make him feel worse? Try simply saying, "Let's get a sponge and clean this up."

I can hear some of you protesting. "Isn't this approach merely coddling? It's a tough world out there. My child has to learn that not everyone is going to be so forgiving or encouraging. I want him to be able to take the knocks too. I want him to be strong." The most effective means of insuring that your child will be "strong" and resilient is for you to inject him with a megadose of self-confidence, with the firm conviction that he is good.

Developing Better Communication with Your Child

There is no substitute for spending time with your child. But then you must make it "quality time." Your child must enjoy being with you, must feel good about himself when he is with you, must see you as someone he can trust. You must become attuned to what is important to your son or daughter.

For younger children, play may be more important than talk in building the foundations of a relationship. Your enthusiasm and connectedness to them while you are dressing a doll, kicking a soccer ball, or buying properties on the Monopoly board are the elements which will draw your child closer. As your children get older, conversation will take on more prominence in strengthening bonds.

There are ways to enhance the communication between you and your child so that your interactions feel more personal, more important.

Despite your best intentions, children resent your lectures or sermons. They tune out and withdraw because they are either bored or they anticipate critical judgment. Younger children will enjoy answering questions because you are demonstrating your interest in them. Older children are likely to be more wary of your probing as they feel an invasion of their privacy. Even your benign inquiries may feel like an interrogation to a fourteen-year-old.

Instead of attempting contact with questions, try self-disclosure. Seize opportunities to tell your child about your work, your childhood, your friends, and your feelings. In addition to enabling your child to get to know you better as a person and not simply a father, appropriate self-disclosures demonstrate your willingness to be open. You will also implicitly be teaching your child how to speak about more personal subjects.

Questioning generates a feeling of a hierarchical relationship. ("I'm in charge here. I'll ask the questions.") Self-disclosure promotes feelings of mutuality. Research in the area of interpersonal communication clearly indicates that self-disclosure by one party significantly increases the probability of self-disclosure by the other. Feelings of familiarity and safety are produced by a pattern of mutual disclosure.

The area of sexuality provides a good illustration of my point. You can encourage greater openness in your teenager if you self-disclose about your own feelings or experiences. I do not necessarily mean revelations about your relationship with your wife, but perhaps about your perceptions, attitudes, or relationships when you were your child's age.

Whenever I speak to a group about the importance of talking

with your adolescent about sex, there are several parents who admit, "I've never been able to do that," and then ask, "How can I begin now?" My answer is always the same. You can't expect your adolescent to be open with you about the most intimate aspect of his or her life if there has not been a close, trusting relationship already established. If you wish to insure that your son or daughter will be able to speak with you about anxiety-producing or painful or sensitive aspects of his or her life, you must begin that dialogue now.

Loving Your Children When They Disappoint You

Unfortunately, many parents only give their children conditional love. "I love you when you _____," or "I will love you if you _____." A bargain is struck, a quid pro quo arrangement is enforced. All too frequently, the child must be the way the parent needs him to be in order to receive approval. Because children crave their parents' love, they will try to respond to these external demands. Along the way, however, they lose the ability to hear their own voices, attend to their psychological needs, or act according to their proclivities. They lose the ability to establish a clear sense of who they are and who they want to become as they focus too intently on pleasing you.

They may also develop an excessive need for approval which further causes them to attune their behavior and preferences to the demands of others. As adults, they procrastinate as they fear making the wrong choice. As adults, they cling to toxic relationships because their sense of self is so tied to the recognition of another. As adults, they feel bound by social conventions and anxiously obsess about what others may think of them. As adults, they remain in an unsatisfying job for a lifetime, unable to discern where their natural gifts truly lie or unable to assert the importance of those gifts. They are unable to act according to their uniqueness. She tries to be the good girl you wanted her to be. He becomes the dutiful son you molded.

You must encourage your child's inclinations. You must encourage your child's ability to choose. You must give them increasing latitude to make decisions for themselves as they mature. You must restrain your impulses to select for them.

As parents, we have many fantasies which we hope our children will fulfill. These fantasies may be specific (e.g., "I hope she wants to play the piano." "I hope she wants to become a physician.") or more general (e.g., "I hope she is a happy person."). All of our fantasies, however, reflect our own needs. They, therefore, do not necessarily respect the aptitudes or desires of our children. Even a general notion such as "I want my child to be happy," often reflects our hopes for the kind of person our child will become, for we reflexively assume that what makes us happy would make our son or daughter happy as well, which, of course, may not be the case, at all.

Allow me to offer a few wishes which parents can have for their children which are completely unintrusive and unselfish. This short list may also help in placing your other hopes and concerns for your children in proper perspective.

I hope my child will be able to love himself.
I hope my child will be able to love others.
I hope my child will be a kind and compassionate person.
I hope my child will have the confidence to do her best.

Try adding two or three other elements to your wish list, but remember that they must respect your child's freedom and individuality.

_____

_____

_____

As you review the combined wish lists, you will note that all of the hoped for qualities can be influenced by how your child perceives you to be living your life. Like father, like child. *One way to love your children is to give them an example they can live by.*

Physical Aspects of Love

You come to parenting with your personality already in place. Perhaps your parents were never physically affectionate, and so that kind of behavior now feels awkward and alien to you. Like most new activities, however, the more you engage in physical affection, the more comfortable you will become with it.

Your child also comes with her own personality. My first daughter, Rachel, was always unusually sensitive to any stimulation. She was the infant who had great difficulty falling asleep and remaining asleep. Because of her extreme sensitivity, Rachel experienced sustained touching as unpleasant. She has never been a cuddler. We may watch television sitting next to one another on the couch, but she does not want me to put my arm around her. That would make her uncomfortable. My second daughter, Sarah, on the other hand, was always more placid, more easygoing than Rachel. She's a big cuddler and loves, for example, to fall asleep pressed up against me or her mother.

Touch is an elixir. Do not inhibit your spontaneous urges to be physically affectionate with your children. Babies who are deprived of touch can actually die. Adults crave touch too. (Some are anxious at the prospect of touch but crave it, nonetheless.) If you affectionately touch your children, they will more fully enjoy the pleasures of touch when they are adults. They will also be more likely to provide your grandchildren with the warmth of their embrace. Get into a routine of touching or hugging your children. An opportune occasion to build the expectation of physical contact into your relationship with your children is when you leave for work or return at the end of the day. At first, you will have to ask for it: "I need a hug before I leave." After a while, even though you may still have to make your request explicit, everyone will anticipate the routine and, therefore, feel less awkward about it.

Needless to say, take advantage of any natural opportunity to even fleetingly touch your child—a pat on the head, an arm around a shoulder, a stroke of a cheek. The contacts will add up, producing a further, clear-cut indication of your love.

Intimacy, Privacy, and Talking About Sex

Questions about sexuality arise in every household. Is it okay to be naked in front of my children? you wonder. By being comfortable with your nakedness, you can communicate that there is nothing shameful, nasty, or disgusting about the human body. Certainly, you can be naked with your son at any age. (Although, during early adolescence, your son may begin to anxiously compare his body to your fully developed one.)

Your daughter, however, may be another matter. As she reaches kindergarten age, she may start to indicate her need for privacy. Suddenly, she wants the door closed when she is undressing, or she may insist that you not look at her when she is in the bath. This should also be a clue that your nudity may begin to make your daughter uncomfortable as she is defining the boundaries of privacy. When she squeals, "Daddy, you're naked!" she is indicating her excitement and her anxiety.

Despite this sudden modesty, your daughter may, nevertheless, express an overt fascination with your body, particularly your penis. She may want to touch it. This will provide you with the opportunity to reinforce the boundaries of privacy. "You can't touch daddy's penis. That's my private part just as you have your private parts which no one else can touch."

There is no need to panic when this occurs, particularly since your daughter may not heed your first admonition and attempt to touch you on other occasions. She is curious about you and your differentness. She is curious about your reactions. She is testing limits. She is indicating her unconscious desire to be intimate with you in a special way. Don't overreact. Just be firm.

There are entire books which address the subject of how to talk to your child about sex. Let me mention some of the frequently noted guidelines:

- Control your own anxiety (and embarrassment) when your child starts asking sexually related questions or when she is running through the house shrieking, "Mommy and daddy are sexing again!"

- Take your cues from your child. Tailor your answers to his conceptual abilities. You may have heard the following related joke. Five year old Andrew approached his mother and asked, "Mommy, can you tell me where I came from?" His mother, having read several child psychology books, takes a deep breath and decides to tackle the question honestly and thoroughly. She launches into a fifteen-minute explanation of the reproductive system, the period of gestation, and the birth process. His eyes glazed over, Andrew replies, "Mom, I just wanted to know where we lived before we moved to Cleveland." Different ages require different levels of discussion.

- Use real terms when talking about anatomy. By using made-up, silly words for vagina or penis, you are implicitly communicating that there is something untoward about those parts of the body.

- All children masturbate. Don't get crazy if you walk in and your son or daughter is stimulating his/her genitals. They do it because they are curious about their bodies and because it feels good. If you don't make a big deal about it, probably neither will they. Your intervention will be required if your child chooses to masturbate in public. At that point, it is certainly appropriate to say, "That's a private activity. We don't do that in the company of other people."

- The more knowledgeable you are about the anatomy and physiology of sexual functioning, the more effective you will be in responding to the sexual issues of your children as they arise.

- The more comfortable you are about your own sexuality, the more comfortable you will be addressing your child's sexual concerns.

- The closer the relationship you have with your child, the more likely he will be to discuss his sexual concerns with you.

- The more you attempt to hide the fact that you are a sexual being from your child, the less likely he will be to find you the appropriate person with whom he can discuss sexual matters.

- How you react to your child's early confrontations with nudity and sexual exploration will have a long-lasting impact on her attitudes and feelings about bodies and sex in general.

- If your child grows up in a home where there is a complete lack of reference to sex, he may infer that sex is a taboo, that sex causes shame and embarrassment. If you want to communicate that sex is a healthy, natural part of a love relationship, do not hide the fact that you and your wife are sexual beings.

The Boundaries of Physical Affection

We were all startled during the past ten years at increasing evidence of the prevalence of the sexual abuse of children. While it is impossible to know the exact magnitude of the problem because most of those who are abused either bury the memory of these encounters or fail to report them, the numbers appear staggering. A new public consciousness has prodded mental health professionals to explore the possibility of its occurrence in their patients. Knowledge of the effects of sexual abuse has allowed victims who had repressed the trauma to understand the links between their ongoing mistrust of others, their aversion to the touch of others, their inability to become emotionally intimate with others, and their childhood experiences.

Hard core abusers, those who feel inadequate relating to other adults and who, therefore, turn to children, are usually compulsive in their behavior. They are frightened, angry individuals who, without professional assistance, will continue to abuse. And while they may rationalize their abuse ("I'm just loving her," or "She enjoyed it too."), deep down inside, most of them know that what they are doing is wrong. But there are many others who have no understanding that their seemingly benign grabbing, patting, or watching of a child (particularly an older one) may cause great discomfort for that child. These individuals need to have their sensitivity to the effects of their actions raised, and they need to stop whatever physical behavior might make a child uncomfortable.

With an increase in your awareness of the possible feelings which various kinds of physical contact with your child may engender, you will learn to be able to act on certain impulses and stifle others. Take your cues from your child. Be responsive to their verbal protestations or nonverbal indications of discomfort or awkwardness. Take them seriously, don't brush them off.

Within these guidelines, do not stop being affectionate with your child because you are afraid of being accused of child molestation. For if you withdraw your physical displays of affection, your child may believe there is something wrong with being affectionate in that manner. And if you stop hugging your child, you will miss the opportunity to enhance, in a very primal way, the bond between the two of you.

How do you know if you are being sexually abusive? Childhood sexual abuse includes any interaction between a child and an adult in which the child is being used as an object of gratification for any of the sexual needs or desires of that adult.

Most fathers know the difference between an affectionate hug and a sexual one. Nevertheless, feelings can be confusing. For example, you may find yourself experiencing sexual stirrings or flashes of attraction toward your daughter. In this case, a guilty reaction is beside the point, as the phenomenon is a very common and almost natural one. What is important is that you resist those impulses. You have been entrusted with the care of this very special person, your daughter. A violation of that trust will have profound ramifications for her.

The Love Vitamin

Loving should be daily. And it should also be explicit.

I admit it. Sometimes, I embarrass my daughter, Sarah. Everyday, I ask her the same question, "How much does daddy love you?" When she was preverbal, I supplied the answer, "A lot," or "A lot, a lot, a lot, a lot." Since that time, she has been capable of providing the response. Sometimes she impishly grins and shrieks, "A lot." Then, I say, "Is that all?" She picks up her cue and continues, "A lot, a lot, a lot, a lot." Sometimes, when I ask the question, she rolls her eyes back in her head, and protests, "Not again, dad." I'm clearly exasperating her (at least superficially).

A small price to pay, I figure.

Keep in mind that most of the skills I have mentioned in this chapter (e.g., verbal loving, physical loving, listening, self-disclosure, empathy) can be applied with your wife or any other person with whom you would like to have a more emotionally intimate relationship. All of us are alike in fundamental ways. We have the same fears, the same insecurities. And, whether we are six, sixteen, or sixty-six, we all want to feel cared about and valued. We all want to have relationships where we can be more trusting and more open. We all want to feel closer to those we love. Your children offer you an unparalleled opportunity to learn to create the kind of relationships you want.

CHAPTER THREE

How to Be More Patient with Your Children

Your six-year-old accidentally knocks over her juice during dinner. Instead of saying, "Let's get a sponge and clean it up," you react: "You're always so clumsy. Can't you do anything right? How many times do I have to tell you to watch your drink at the table? If you had taken a nap like you were supposed to, you wouldn't be so tired, and this wouldn't have happened." You then may turn to your wife and continue: "She's sitting next to you. Didn't you see that the glass was near her elbow and she was going to knock it over eventually?" It's called overkill.

But whatever we might label the outburst—inappropriate, excessive, unreasonable, irrational, or abusive—it reflects a tired, stressed-out, angry, unhappy person. It is difficult to be any of these and still be a good father. Your resentments inevitably spill over onto your loved ones. Your children, who are entitled to your patience and understanding, instead receive the products of your uncontrollable frustrations. Conversely, when you are more content at work, with your spouse, and in your relationships with significant others, you are likely to be more easy-going, even-tempered, tolerant, and compassionate with your children.

Our society places a premium on being an optimistic person. You are not supposed to show your unhappiness to the world, so you apply a mask, a happy face, when you leave your home. "Hi, how are you?" "Fine. How are you?" "Fine." The charade is repeated on countless occasions every day. But you drop the mask when you walk through your front door in the evening. The real you emerges. The frustrated you emerges.

When you are feeling extremely deprived or stressed, you are always functioning on the edge. You may be able to retain a certain equanimity when all is going smoothly, but you lose your composure at the slightest obstacles. In your reaction, you are unable to distinguish between minor, harmless glitches which are to be expected, and more serious occurrences. When you are overloaded, you bellow orders and make impetuous decisions based on black-and-white perceptions. Insignificant snags take on crisis proportions. Your manner produces an atmosphere of anxiety, and you frighten your children in the process.

Oftentimes, you even believe you are relaxed. But, then, you find yourself snapping at your child or throwing your book down in disgust at the slightest disruption. This, of course, is a warning signal, telling you how tightly wound up you really are.

You feel unable to express your anger toward your employer, so you lash out at your family members. You feel so little control in your work environment, so you act more autocratically at home. You feel unable to confront your parents, so your anger seeps out toward others whom you love. You wish to avoid another fight with your wife, but your resentment is displaced onto your children.

Your children serve as convenient targets because they feel least threatening. You feel safe in venting your emotions toward them because they cannot retaliate. Most likely, you are not even cognizant of the fact that you are taking out your frustrations and disappointments on your children. When you reflexively erupt at them, stop and ask yourself, "Why am I picking on an eight-year-old? What or who am I really upset about?"

It is commonplace for a child to temporarily hate his father (or mother). You are bound periodically to frustrate what he experiences as super important. It is also not unusual for fathers (or mothers) to experience flashes of hatred toward their children. But *you* are not a six-year-old. You have more perspective. You have more mature mechanisms for coping with frustration. So when your anger feels so intense, take a time-out. Examine your life. Why are you feeling so frustrated? What are the feelings just engendered by your child's behavior piggybacking on? What "buttons" has your child pushed?

I feel like I don't have any control over my life.

I feel so inadequate.

I feel so disappointed in everyone.

I feel so unloved.

I feel so unappreciated.

I feel so unimportant.

If any of the above statements describe how you feel, you are probably not a happy individual. Any one of the above statements can profoundly affect your view of yourself and your life. All of them usually have their origin in old, childhood frustrations and feelings of deprivation. They are, therefore, difficult to reverse and will probably necessitate professional assistance. It is not easy for most men to admit emotional difficulties and ask for guidance from another. But, in this case, you must.

Of course, some of the seeds of your impatience and anger toward your child were planted when he first entered the picture. At the same time you were thrilled, you also experienced greater stress and frustration as your life changed in so many fundamental ways: There were more responsibilities, there were new financial pressures, your wife paid you less attention, you were forced to give up some of your narcissism, there was less marital communication, your sexual relationship changed dramatically, your life became child-oriented as opposed to adult-oriented, you were tired much of the time, there was more marital conflict, it felt like you and your wife were no longer lovers.

You have received a great deal from your child, but you have also had to cope with all of these changes, these deprivations. Change, in and of itself, of course, is unsettling. Some fathers cope well and adjust fairly effortlessly to their new circumstances. But others don't. What can you do to cope more effectively with your feelings of responsibility, stress, and deprivation?

You must first become aware of your feelings and articulate them. You need not be ashamed to admit that you occasionally think, "I wish things were the way they were before Billy arrived," or even, "I sometimes wish Billy were not here."

The second step is to see where you can reduce the stress in other areas of your life and make a plan to do so. Have you taken on too many commitments? Does your life-style reflect your financial means, or are you in over your head? Have you left enough time just for you? Have you incorporated any physical exercise into your routine? Are you continually assessing the balance in your life between what you *should* be doing and what you *want* to be doing? Are you getting enough sleep?

The third step is to talk with your wife about how you both can insure that you do not lose the intimacy of your marriage. While it may require more effort and ingenuity, especially when your children are young, there is no reason for either romance or sex to disappear from the relationship. You and your wife must also feel as though you are a team. If one of you is feeling inordinate stress at a particular time, the other must assist in any way they can to help reduce the pressure.

You must be in an open enough, relaxed enough frame of mind so that you can derive maximum joy from your interactions with your child. Only then will you feel truly pleased about your ability to bypass some of your needs for the good of your child. Only then will it seem as though what you have given up is relatively unimportant when compared to how your life has been enhanced by the arrival of your son or daughter.

Understanding What's Bothering Your Child

My eight year old daughter, Rachel, had just read me an essay she had written for school. "What do you think?" she inquired. "I think it's very interesting. It might become even more interesting if you told us more about how the main character feels." Tears immediately welled up in her eyes. She slammed her pencil down. "You never think anything I do is good! I don't even know why I bother to ask!" Sobbing, she then ran up to her room, and slammed the door shut.

I give Rachel a great deal of praise. I knew, therefore, that her reaction, her abject feelings of rejection were unwarranted. I also knew that my feedback had been supportive and gentle. So Rachel's reaction was unreasonable, excessive. And that was my clue that something else was really going on, that my comment had touched an open wound. Sure enough, when my wife came down to ask what all the hysteria had been about, the missing element between my benign comment and my daughter's reaction was clarified. Rachel's best friend, Natalie, had been busy with other activities all week. And earlier in the day, when Rachel had telephoned Natalie, Natalie hurriedly informed Rachel that she couldn't talk because Marjorie (Rachel's rival for Natalie's affection) was playing over at her house. Consequently, Rachel was "primed" for further feelings of rejection.

From the outset, my younger daughter, Sarah, was temperamentally easy-going. Unperturbed by frustrating circumstances, she easily moved on to other activities. When she was able to verbalize, any request I made of her was met with a cheerful, "Okay, daddy." With the arrival of her baby brother, however, Sarah turned into a different child. Whining, pouting, fits of temper were triggered by innocuous privations. But, of course, Sarah was feeling overwhelmingly deprived. She felt displaced, replaced, and forgotten because of the presence of a new competitor for her parents' affection. Oftentimes, the beginning of this "uncharacteristic" behavior we see in our child can be directly traced to the arrival of a newborn.

Just as your frustrations and resentments are often displaced onto your children, your children will often shower you with outbursts which your behavior does not warrant. It is when their reaction seems most unreasonable (and often most offensive to you) that you do not have the luxury of simply reacting ("Don't you speak that way to me! Go to your room now!"). Instead, this is your cue to investigate further and piece together the antecedents of your child's explosion.

A child's development is an *ongoing* process. Because we understood our daughter's anxieties, insecurities, and conflicts when she was six years old does not imply an understanding of our daughter who is now sixteen. She is an evolving person and her needs will change. Therefore, we can never assume that we understand our child "because that's the way she is and that's the way she'll always be." As she moves through different stages, new issues and concerns will inevitably arise—and new "understandings" must accompany this dynamic process.

However, when you already feel like you are at your own limit of stress and unhappiness, you will not want to think about the causes of your child's obnoxious behavior. And even if you do muster the patience to investigate further before simply reacting, you may still think, "I don't care why! I just can't take it. She shouldn't be allowed to get away with this!" You don't have the room for compassion because you already feel overwhelmed while trying to cope with your own frustrations.

If you are going to become a more effective parent, you must become a happier person as well. You must do something to rectify the sources of dissatisfaction in your life instead of allowing them to eat away at you. And you must insure that, in some instances, you put your own needs first.

How to Love Your Children When They Are Complete Brats

It is easy to love your mate or your child when things are going smoothly, when the others are being the way you want them to be. You readily love them when they are acting in a lovable manner (i.e., when they are fulfilling your needs). The acid test of an adult-adult or an adult-child relationship is not whether the two individuals can get along well or have fun together. What distinguishes those relationships which really work from those which simmer with resentment or result in alienation from one another is the dyad's ability to (1) resolve conflict constructively and (2) respond nondefensively and nonpunitively to the other's expression of anger. Instead of escalating, retaliating, making excuses, or offering rationalizations, these individuals really listen. They try to understand the other's feelings. They attempt to find mutually satisfying solutions.

When your child says, "I hate you," your impulse is to punish, to show him who is boss, to demand respect. ("You can't talk to your father that way.") Because your child's comment seems so egregious, you feel as though he should not be allowed "to get away with it." As difficult as it may be, however, you must control your anger and dismay. You must step back and understand why someone who loves you and who desperately wants your love in return would let loose with something so "dangerous."

Help your child translate his verbal and behavioral outbursts into feeling statements. "I know you're angry because I wouldn't let you _____," or "I know you feel it was unfair of me to _____. Let me explain again why I didn't think it was a good idea." Your comment may not be appreciated at that very moment, but it will be heard. Your child may still believe you treated him unfairly, but he will know you understand and have considered his feelings. To reiterate our discussion of empathy from Chapter Two, never underestimate the power of your child feeling understood by you.

Too many parents are unable to see things from their children's perspective. Too many parents do not appreciate how often children feel unheard by them. Too many parents, unfortunately, have "pushed" their children away by their lack of empathy.

Is it ever okay to express my anger toward my child? you may wonder. Of course it is. But like praise, angry statements must not be aimed at your child's *character*. ("How could you be so stupid?" or "Don't you know how to listen?" or "Can't you ever act responsibly?" or "Do you always have to be so selfish?") You can express your anger about your child's *behavior*. You should also include an explanation for your anger in your expression. You want to communicate that there are legitimate reasons for your anger, and you want to tell your child "how to do it right" or "how to do it better" the next time. Ultimately, you are also implicitly teaching your child how to express his own anger in an acceptable manner.

> "It makes me angry when I have to tell you to do something so many times. It makes me feel that what I want is not important to you."
>
> "I'm angry because you promised to do that and you didn't keep your promise."
>
> "I'm angry because we all have our own responsibilities in the house and you didn't uphold yours. We can't keep a house in running condition without each of us doing his part."
>
> "I got angry because I trusted you to watch your little brother when you said you would. Instead, you wandered off to play in your room. It also frightens me because he's little and could hurt himself."

For some fathers, frustration and anger boil over into rage and result in obviously abusive behavior. Out of control, they hit, they launch into a frightening tirade, they say hurtful things. They often "automatically" inflict the same treatment they received from their own fathers. Other fathers, sensing that they are about to lose control, manage to withdraw and, thereby, spare the children their wrath. They leave the room until they have calmed down. They ask themselves, What is *really* bothering me? They count to ten. They remind themselves that their child is only a child. A helpful suggestion: Never make a decision about punishment when you are enraged. You will then avoid an excessive edict which you would want to retreat from at a later time.

You must get a handle on your anger (no matter what the source), because your children will inevitably present you with ongoing challenges. Children will always test your limits. This natural testing process is an ingredient in the development of their autonomy and an identity separate from you. What can *I* do? is your child's underlying premise. What can I get away with? is her ongoing concern. In order to help your child set reasonable and safe limits, your understanding, guidance, and patience are essential.

Before You Walk in the Door

A child also needs the freedom to act his or her age. You must, therefore, be prepared for the constant noise, self-injury due to carelessness and/or the desire to explore her environment, bouts of whining and pouting, unreasonable demands, and uncontrollable outbursts. If you already feel maximally stressed, none of this will be tolerable. You will overreact to a natural course of events.

Fathers often tell me, "I wish I could just have twenty minutes to myself after I come home so I could unwind before being assaulted by my kids." "It won't work," I reply. Your children feel like they have not seen you in a long time. (It may not seem that long a time to you.) Your wife is also anxious to unload some of her child-care burden.

If you walk in at the end of your workday and say to your child, "I need to do some things. I'll be with you in a few minutes," you will have set in motion a negative dynamic because of the messages you are implicitly communicating. "I'm not that excited to see you," or "You're another chore that I will get to." You may not hear a word of protest but stop and notice how quickly the excited, expectant look on your child's face vanishes.

You must be ready for your children when you cross the threshold of your front door. You must "be all there" and not preoccupied. You must reciprocate their enthusiasm. You must communicate that you are happy to see them, not only by your words, but by your behavior as well. Children do not feel important to their father when he looks through his mail before he looks at them.

It is understandable that you would feel a need to decompress after a grueling day, topped off, perhaps, by an agonizing commute home. But you must do it before you reunite with your family. There is a simple relaxation exercise which will assist you in not only reducing your tension but in focusing on the present. Close your eyes. Beginning with your toes and moving up your body, you will tense those muscles as tightly as possible, hold that tension for five seconds, and slowly release it. Then repeat. Hold the tension in your toes for five seconds and slowly release it. After your toes, move to your feet. Next, your calves, your thighs, your buttocks, your stomach, your chest, your fists, your arms, your chest, your shoulders, your mouth, and, last, your forehead. Concentrate all of your attention on each part as you tense and relax it. Don't let your mind wander. You should feel relaxed, refreshed, and alert by the end of the exercise. If you drive home, another possibility is to pull off on a side street for a few minutes and listen to relaxing music and/or do the above relaxation exercise. If you walk home from a train or bus, buy a tape player and listen to an enjoyable tape.

Anything you do which relieves the stress in your life will enable you to be a more patient parent. There are dozens of stress-reducing techniques which are readily available. Find one or two which work for you. Whether it be physical exercise to relieve tension and provide more energy, meditation to help you relax and remain focused on the present, or better time management which will reduce your sense of ongoing pressure, the effects of activities and plans designed to make you feel better will spill over into your role as father. And you will have the additional dividend of feeling as though you are doing something for yourself as well as your child.

When you find that you have become more patient, you will

probably notice that you are generally happier and more contented as well. Your ability to be more patient will make your child feel more loved, valued, and understood. And that will make you feel like a more successful father and a better human being.

CHAPTER FOUR

How to Enjoy Your Children More

David Horton, a thirty-six-year-old manager of an upscale retail clothing store, had been playing basketball, his favorite pastime, with his son once a week for the past four years. When David's daughter, Melanie, reached the age of five, he decided to prove that he was not in the least sexist. One Saturday morning, with obvious enthusiasm, he invited Melanie to accompany him to the courts down the street from their home. "I'll teach you how to play basketball just like I taught Robbie. It'll be a lot of fun," he promised her.

Melanie agreed to the outing because she wanted the opportunity to spend time with her dad. But she had no interest in basketball, and once on the court, she clearly indicated to her father that she was simply going through the motions. As Melanie's indifference continued, David's enthusiasm predictably waned. By the end of their hour together, both father and daughter were feeling less than pleased about their interaction.

David's ardor for his preferences kept him from first considering his daughter's interests. And in his desire to treat his children equitably, he lost sight of their individual differences. Melanie's passion, as it turns out, is modern dance. The question for David then becomes: Am I man enough, open enough, free enough to enjoy modern dancing with my daughter?

Not only did David's focus on his own desires preclude him from anticipating those of Melanie, but he also failed to place himself in her frame of reference. No five-year-old is going to enjoy an activity which she is unable to master or cope with because of her undeveloped musculature (not to mention that she was a little too short to reach the basket). Dancing was something which gave Melanie a sense of accomplishment, a sense of mastery. It was literally thrilling for her to move languidly and fluidly to a piece of music.

It is imperative that you try to adopt your child's perspective. For example, because you have continuously been bombarded with more mail than you would like for many years, it may not occur to you that it might be exciting for your youngster to receive a letter from you. Pulling weeds in your backyard is, generally, a grimy, sweaty, unpleasant affair. But your child would probably love to get dirty, be outside, and feel a sense of accomplishment. What other commonplace activities have you overlooked which your child might enjoy?

_____

_____

_____

_____

_____

_____

_____

_____

_____

Learning to Love the Process

Most men are outcome-oriented as opposed to process-oriented. They define objectives, keep their eyes on the target, and focus on its accomplishment. Deriving pleasure from the journey to the end result is, at best, of secondary interest. Men also tend not to enjoy an activity unless they excel at it or unless they win. Children, on the other hand, tend to concentrate more on the process. Is this fun? Is this exciting? These are the measuring sticks they live by. I recently had to interrupt building a Lego house with my four-year-old daughter because we had to go shopping. I was surprised at how easily Sarah was prepared to relinquish the activity. Apparently, she had had her fun and was, therefore, simply pleased with what had transpired. Completion of the house was not necessary. She was ready to move on. Clearly, what was most important to Sarah was that we had embarked on an activity *together*.

You tell your five-year-old to choose a book for you to read to her before bedtime. She reacts with excitement and anticipation of the beautiful pictures, interesting story, and the time to feel close to you. She hands you the book she has chosen, and if you are like many fathers, you immediately look to see how many pages are involved and calculate the time required to get through it. "What is the task and when will it end?" is your approach.

Let me offer an alternative strategy. Instead of reading straight through the book, ask your child questions about the story along the way. What do you think is going to happen? What do you wish the character would do next? Did you ever feel that way? Why do you think the character is doing that? How does the story make you feel? Tell your child a personal incident in your own life which may be related to the themes of the story. When did something like that happen to you? When did you feel that way? Seize the opportunity to (1) stimulate your child's imagination, (2) learn more about your child, (3) allow your child to learn more about you, and (4) build a stronger bond between the two of you.

Play is an opportunity for more than teaching your child how to do it right. Play is an opportunity for more than fun. Play provides an opportunity for significant physical and emotional contact. Play allows both of you to give, to receive, to share a sense of accomplishment, to communicate love, to indicate interest in the other, to be affectionate. Play furnishes both of you with the occasion to be spontaneous, to be silly, to be free. Play should never be transformed into serious business.

Don't always be *instructing* when you are playing with your child. It is certainly appropriate to ask, "Would you like me to show you how to _____?" (This is particularly true with older children who may want to enhance their ability, while your four-year-old will find enjoying himself to be a sufficient goal.) But avoid the mind-set of viewing every interaction with your child as an occasion to teach him something. Play is supposed to be fun, not another skill or subject which your son believes he must learn. This is not school!

Your children present you with an opportunity to reclaim your playfulness. For too many men, "life is serious business" *all the time*. They feel they must always be productive, always be competent. Even when they "play," they become caught up in doing well, being competitive, proving themselves. Instead of feeling enthusiastic, they simply feel *intense*. Enjoy your play. Enjoy the freedom. Teach your child about enthusiasm, not about winning.

Games implicitly teach our children anyway. They are vehicles for understanding the importance of incremental learning. They reinforce persistence. They force greater eye and motor coordination. They require coping with frustration. Play builds body and character. But above all, play must be fun. This must be the message which you communicate to your child by your own approach and attitude.

Being Silly

I don't know about you, but there are few things in life that give me greater pleasure than seeing my child laugh. Get down with your children, especially your infant, your toddler, and your preschooler. Use nonsense syllables, make funny noises, see how many contorted positions you can push your face into. Drop your adult posture for the time being. Let your inner child take center stage again.

Even though they may mock embarrassment, your older children will also enjoy your silliness. Your childlike behavior will contrast with your adult role of authority and, therefore, allow your son or daughter to perceive you to be accessible. They will be more likely to believe you can understand their desires and frustrations because you've shown a childlike side of yourself. And they will be pleased to see how the two of you are alike.

Don't limit your roughhousing to your son or you will miss out on your daughter's squeals of delight. Girls, too, will love the excitement and the physical contact. Remember that roughhousing also provides the occasion for expressions of affection (e.g., hugging, laughing). And you do not want to communicate to your daughters that they are fragile figurines, incapable of safely emerging from vigorous physical contact. If your child is hurt during rough play, that should not be a signal to cease that activity forever. Simply see what you could have done differently in order to increase the safety of the situation for the future. (Some children, of course, will find roughhousing frightening or too intense. However, they will probably find a less strenuous activity—a horsey ride, a shoulder ride—to be pleasurable, nonetheless.)

When engaging in physical games with their children, fathers are often prone to make sure they give their children "a workout." Or they are particularly keen on helping their children "build character." This approach invariably injects a seriousness into the play which detracts from its enjoyable potential. At its worst, the intensity escalates as you lose control of your need to prove your manliness and prowess. When playing with your child, you want the interaction to be a pleasurable one. You don't want it to turn into a lesson or a trial by fire.

Your child will derive more pleasure from your interactions if you are obviously having a good time. "I had a great time playing soccer with you today," will be savored by him. The game will have provided the opportunity for him to give you something. It will have also offered proof that being together with you is a *mutually* satisfying experience.

The Zen of Fatherhood

If you're like most of us, you have a lot on your mind. And while you may not qualify for the clinical label of obsessive type, you may find that your mind always wanders back to an unfinished project at work, an upcoming meeting, a plan to clear up a financial predicament, or a risk whose outcome you anxiously await. You are always feeling the pressure of time as well. There never seems to be enough of it, so you are invariably pushing yourself through the present task so that you can get to the next one. "Savoring the moment" is not a part of your life-style.

Your child is sensitive to your degree of engagement with him. He will know if you are in a rush to get through with him so you can get back to what you really want to do. He can tell if you are not all there. He will resent it when he only receives your divided attention, because you will, once again, be indicating that he is not important to you. On the other hand, he will bask when you prove your singular interest in him.

You, too, will lose when you are distracted. You will lose the potential of that moment, that interaction, which can never be recovered. When you set aside time with your child, make sure you are completely present during that occasion. You must let go of the rest of your life for that period. If you have difficulty being completely in the here and now, it will help to remain focused on your child. Really listen to him. Listen to how his mind works. Watch him. Revel in his uniqueness. When there is a lull in the conversation, wonder about him. Ask yourself questions about him. How does he feel about himself? How does he feel about his ability to _____? How does he feel about me?

Eastern traditions have always emphasized the importance of "being in the now." A "present orientation" precludes anxiety about what lies ahead, what tasks need completion, what responsibilities need your attention. By being completely present, you can rid yourself of all the worries which you cannot do anything about at that moment anyway. You will, thereby, inevitably feel freer and more relaxed.

Wives often describe similar shortcomings in their husbands. "He's always preoccupied." "I can tell he's not really listening to me." "He's not interested in hearing how I truly feel." She also, therefore, feels as though she is unimportant to you. The lessons learned from being focused with your child should generalize to your marital relationship. When you are completely in the present with your family members, all of you will benefit.

Special Time

"I spend a lot of time with my family," Gary, a thirty-one year old father of three tells me. "He really does," his wife, Helen, supportively adds. Then, why is nine year old Brian, Helen's son from a previous marriage, feeling so unloved and alienated from the family?

One year after Gary and Helen were married, they had a set of beautiful twin girls. Around the same time as the birth of the twins, Brian's father moved a thousand miles away in order to remarry and begin a new life. As we might have predicted, Brian reacted to all of these changes and displacements with increasing feelings of rejection and abandonment. He became rebellious, seemingly defying his parents at every step of the way. When his concerned mother tried to find out from Brian what was going on, she was met with an uncommunicative but emphatic, "Nothing!" or "I don't want to talk about it!" or "Just leave me alone!"

It quickly became apparent to me that Brian desperately needed to feel reassured that he was still important. Brian desperately needed to feel loved again. "How much time do you spend with Brian?" I asked his stepfather. "I spend a lot of time with my family," he replied. Indeed, Gary did spend a considerable amount of time with his family, but Gary did not spend any *special time* with Brian. Gary did not spend the individual time with Brian required to reassure him that he had not lost his family, that he was important to his parents, and that he was an integral member of this newly reconstituted household.

Family outings are great. They generate a sense of cohesion, a sense of being a unit. But you must remember that you have a relationship with each of your children. Each of them has different needs. Each of them wants a unique bond with you. Each of them desires a particular place in your heart. "Spending time with the kids" is fine, but you must also be mindful of having *individual* time with each son and daughter. Every one of us, child and adult alike, wants to feel special to those we dearly love. Each of us wants to be reassured.

Appreciating Your Children

Children provide fathers with countless rewards. They can make you laugh. They can surprise you with their perceptiveness and blatant honesty. They can amaze you with their imaginativeness and creativity. They can enable you to see the world anew by their sense of wonder. They can serve as models of freedom by witnessing their spontaneity. They can make you feel important by their adoration.

You will appreciate your children most when you provide them with openings to demonstrate their capacities. Take the time to ask them open-ended questions. "What do you think would happen if _____?" "Why do you think some people _____ and other people _____?" Take the time to follow up on statements spontaneously made by your children with questions designed to draw them out further, instead of simply responding, "Uh-huh." You will not only be stimulating their thought processes, but you will have another opportunity to understand how they view the world. The answers they offer will provide more insights into how their minds work and how they interpret events in their universe.

Your child is ripe for fun. She will react appreciatively to your unexpectedly going out of your way to make her feel special. Observe the anticipation and excitement in your child when you pass her a secret note at dinner which reads, "Meet me in the den at 7:00 so we can plan a surprise for your mom's birthday. Don't tell anyone else about this."

You can view your children as a nuisance, a bother, and an onerous responsibility. When they then inevitably disrupt your world, you can react by thinking, "There he goes, being a brat again." Or you can view your child as a precious vessel whose potential as a human being you can maximize through your nurturance and guidance. You can remain preoccupied with your personal frustrations or you can focus more of your attention on your child's needs. You can "put in time" with your children, or you can actively enjoy all they have to offer. You can simply fulfill your obligations to them, or you can expend the energy required to understand them. You can maintain an autocratic, parent-child distance from them, or you can invite a close, mutually satisfying relationship.

Oftentimes, fathers spend more time with their children because they believe that is what they should do *for their children*. But fathers should become more engaged with their sons and daughters because of what it can do for them as well. Our children can provide us with new experiences and evoke emotions which we have long since lost touch with. Our children can provide us with a joyfulness that has been buried by an adulthood of responsibilities. Our children can provide us with vehicles for the caring and closeness which most of us so yearn for.

CHAPTER FIVE

How to Find More Time for Your Children

When was the last time you took an unscheduled day off from work just so you could spend the time playing with your children? When was the last time you left work *one hour* early just so you could be with your son or daughter? In other words, when was the last time you made an unexpected statement about what is truly important in your life?

Taking Stock

Most of us are busy, too busy. We feel as though we are on a treadmill, going from responsibility to responsibility, wearily attempting to keep up with all we have to do. Our lives have developed routines which we fulfill. Oftentimes, however, *these schedules feel as though they are happening to us.* We do not deliberately choose to act in certain ways as much as we seem to shuffle in the direction in which we are pointed. We seldom sit down and assess what is really important because our priorities seem to have been programmed a long time ago.

On countless occasions, you have sighed, "I just can't do everything." And you were right. Perhaps you can hurriedly rush through everything for a period, all the time deriving little satisfaction from anything. You certainly cannot do *everything* in a relaxed manner which will maximize your effectiveness and pleasure in life. It is time to take stock so that you can focus on the important and not be distracted by the insignificant.

There are 168 hours in the week. Eliminating approximately fifty hours per week for sleep, twenty hours per week for eating, and three hours a week for grooming, you are left with ninety-five precious hours. Now, consider how you spend that time and how you would actually *like* to spend that time.

Make a chart. In the left-hand column, write your usual activities—work, commuting, spending time with friends, spending time with extended family, spending time with your wife, playing with your children, fixing things around the house, grocery shopping, religious activities, and any others which are a part of your routine. In the second column, note the number of hours you expend on each of them during a typical week. In the third column, write the number of hours you would ideally like to spend on each category during a typical week.

ACTIVITY	ACTUAL HOURS	IDEAL HOURS

At least, now, you have a clear-sighted direction and explicit objectives. You must diminish the difference between your "Actual Hours" and "Ideal Hours" columns. If you are like many men, you may find the most glaring gap is between the actual and desired time you spend with your children. Part of the reason for this is that you believe most of the other items *must* receive your attention, while your children can wait. As a result, many children wait and wait and wait.

Working Overtime

We spend by far the greatest proportion of our waking hours at work. Forty work hours a week is reasonable. Some jobs demand a somewhat greater commitment. But when I see many men spend fifty, sixty, seventy hours or more at their office, I begin to worry—for them and for their children.

Granted, some of these men simply enjoy their work much more than they enjoy their wives, their children, or their leisure. But most of these men are driven by fear. Fear of failure, fear of being homeless, fear of what their colleagues might think of them if they were the first to leave, fear that they won't live up to the expectations of their fathers, fear that they are not man enough.

Michael Hurley, a forty-eight year old neurosurgeon, reckoned that he had been working an average of seventy hours a week for the past ten years. A seven-figure income and professional awards had not been able to quiet his financial insecurities nor his concerns about his status among his peers. "I usually have more patients than I even want," he offered at one of our initial sessions. "Why don't you turn down a few referrals?" I inquired. "I can't. That physician might think I'm too busy and start referring patients elsewhere." Michael lived with the fear that it would all disappear, that he would find himself struggling for patients, for income, for recognition. He was also unmotivated to spend more time at home because of marital dissatisfaction. As a result, of course, his three children saw little of him.

It was not until Michael felt secure within himself and more positive about his marriage that he was able to cut back at his office. Michael's fear of the potential consequences of turning away a new referral will probably never completely disappear. His childhood was surrounded by too much poverty and deprivation for that to occur. But his increasing self-confidence and the greater pleasure he eventually derived from his marriage allowed him more room to breathe.

Some men have profound doubts about their self-worth, and those insecurities create an addiction to their workplace. Driven by alternating moods of excitement and terror, they must prove their value to themselves and others (oftentimes, their fathers). "But, I love my work," these men tell me. "Not true," I point out. "What you love is how you believe your work reflects your importance as a man and as a human being." Which parent or significant other failed to make you feel important and worthy? I wonder. "Workaholics" answer in the affirmative to many of the following questions. Do any apply to you as well?

> Do you think about work even at social events, at the movies, or when you are playing with your children?
>
> Are you unable to really enjoy anything but work?
>
> Do you have difficulty fully concentrating on anything but work?
>
> Do you forgo vacations for years even if you can afford them?
>
> Do you think about work during sex?
>
> Is it difficult for you to feel good when you are not "working" on some task?
>
> Do you view those who work less than you as loafers or unmotivated or unsuccessful or unproductive or wimps?
>
> Is having fun unimportant to you?

Do you believe your children can wait?

Do you believe that you are not really essential to the emotional well-being of your children?

Some men stay at the office longer than is necessary because they want to stay away from home. Perhaps they feel more in control in their work environment, safer in this part of their world. Others go to the gym four nights a week or go out for a drink with their buddies most nights after work in order to avoid intimacy or conflicts with their wives. If problems in your marriage are keeping you away from home, you must resolve those problems so that your children are not denied your presence in the family.

For some men, of course, their only source of self-esteem and, perhaps, therefore, their only source of real satisfaction, is their success in their chosen field of endeavor. "I *have* to put in those kind of hours at the office," is often a disguise for "That's the only place I can feel a sense of accomplishment. That's the only place I can feel good about who I am."

"There's nothing I can do about the long hours at work," fathers often tell me. But this is rarely true. Especially after we examine all of the unconscious fears driving their work schedule. Unfortunately, when we firmly believe we have no choice, no other options, we also feel depressed because of our seemingly impotent position.

"I have to work those hours in order to maintain our life-style," or "I have to put that much time in so we can live the way we would like," are other frequently heard justifications for the dearth of contact with wife and children. The words imbue the individual with a sense of nobility and self-sacrifice. "I'm doing this for you," he tells his family. But when "better life-style" means a bigger house than is necessary, more expensive adult toys, or the ability "to keep up" with others, we have lost sight of not only values, but our loved ones as well. What could be more precious than the time we allot to spend with our sons and daughters? We can only teach when we have established a rela-tionship. How can we ignore opportunities to impart what is right and what is wrong? How can we pass up the chance to instill in our children a sense of self-confidence? What is the price we pay when we direct so much of our energies to "affording a better life-style"?

Messages we received during our formative years also continue to keep us away from our family.

"Your job is to provide for your family."

"You are going to be the best lawyer there ever was."

"Keep your nose to the grindstone if you want to get anywhere."

"There will always be time for fun later. Take advantage of opportunities now."

"First, you have to attain a certain level of security."

All of these communications assume that in order for you to be "successful," you must maintain an unwavering focus on work. (Of course, in reality, we envy those who are "successful" and have a great deal of time for leisure.) But it is up to you to remain clear about what is *really* important and to *act* on that clarity.

Perfection, Procrastination, and Other Time Wasters

Perfectionists have no time for people. They immerse themselves in tasks. They are prisoners to detail. Particularly when children enter your life, you must learn to live with a messy world, a less than orderly existence. The presence of children may require a level of professional development which falls short of your ideal. I live with a constant, nagging level of frustration. There are academic journals I never have a moment to read. As a teacher, I live with the insecurity that perhaps I am not absolutely current with every trend in my field. I must live with the notion that I cannot know everything which might be relevant to my work. And I accept these limitations, because I have adopted a certain perspective:

There are few things worth doing perfectly.
I am a good enough psychologist, teacher, and writer.
I only have a limited amount of time.
It is important to live a balanced life.
There is nothing more important to me than my family.

Some of you do not spend more time at the office than you should, but you get sidetracked from what is truly important nonetheless. Even if you are clear about your family priorities, you are unable to be assertive. You are unable to turn down requests for your time from others. You want to be liked. You want to be seen as a good guy. Perhaps you do not feel as though your needs are as deserving of attention. Whatever the underlying restraints, if you find it difficult to live as you would like, to abide by your priorities, you would likely benefit from assertion training, which teaches individuals how to ask for what they want, how to set limits in relationships, and how to decline a demand or request of another without feeling anxious or guilty about doing so. An excellent assertion training book is *When I Say "No," I Feel Guilty*, by Dr. Manuel Smith.

A myriad of factors may keep you from utilizing your time effectively. Some may be complex and deep-rooted, such as a tendency to procrastination. Others, such as a lack of organizational skills, are more easily tackled. Although procrastination may be muted by retaining your focus on your priorities, it may also require professional assistance in order to resolve the self-doubt, fear of failure, and/or fear of success which fuels it.

If you are like most of us, you spend more time than you would like socializing with certain others. I am not simply referring to social outings or networking which would be "good for business." I am also including acquaintances or some who you even refer to as "friends." You see them out of a sense of obligation or because you have fallen into a pattern or because you do not want to hurt their feelings. ("Every year we go on a July 4th picnic with them." "We always celebrate our anniversaries together because they fall on the same day.") But think about it for a moment. Would you want others spending time with you because they felt obligated to do so?

As hard-pressed as you are for time, you grudgingly spend three to five hours on a typical evening with people toward whom you do not feel any particular affinity. Three to five uninterrupted hours! How often do you spend three to five uninterrupted hours with your spouse or your child? This is not a plea for social isolation from the outside world, but it is a recognition that we must continually make active choices about the time in our lives, active choices based on values and ongoing admissions of what is really important to us.

We tend to postpone our children. "I'll have more time when I finish this project," you promise. But as you know, there will inevitably be another project after this one which will catch your fancy. You will probably live well into your seventies and, perhaps, even beyond. But what if you don't? What if it all ended tomorrow? What have you chosen to put on hold? Your child will never be two again. You will never again have the opportunity to observe his wonder or the amazing explosion of his abilities at this point in his life. That moment will be gone forever.

The Myth of Quality Time

"I make sure I spend fifteen minutes of quality time with my son every evening," a father tells me. "Good," I reply. "It's important to have daily contact with your child. And even if the time period is a brief one, as long as you are focused and concentrated on your child, that time will be valuable."

It has become fashionable and acceptable to speak about "quality time" spent with children. Oftentimes, however, the parent's description of quality time sounds more like "rushed time." The fifteen minutes is squeezed into a parent's and child's busy lives. You commit to spending these precious minutes with your child every evening because you want that contact and realize it is important to your child. But it is taking place at the child's bedtime, when he and you are tired from a long, active day. Knowing how excited your child will be to see you, you perhaps choose to spend that quality time immediately after you come home from work. But you are hungry and distracted by thoughts of dinner or wondering if that letter you were awaiting is lying in that stack of mail.

Your son needs more than "rushed time." Your daughter needs you for more than the fifteen minutes of "quality time" which you devote to her. While we allocate the education of our children to the schools, we must not lose sight of the fact that we, parents, are their primary and most influential teachers. It takes time to effectively, lovingly, and fully answer your child's questions.

"Why can birds fly and not people?"
"Why can my friend Janice go to the party, and I can't?"
"Why do you have to work so much?"
"Is grandma going to die?"
"Is the monster in my dream going to get me?"
"Where do people go when they die?"

It takes time to truly understand your child. As we have become more psychologically minded, we have become conversant with terms such as "separation anxiety," "adolescent rebellion," "the terrible twos," etc. It is easy to apply such a label to a child and feel satisfied that we comprehend the reasons for his behavior. But it would also be insufficient. For what is your *particular* child feeling, thinking, and needing? What about separation frightens her? What exactly is she rebelling against?

It take time to converse with your child in a way which will stimulate her imagination. It takes energy and calm to resist the temptation to simply answer, "Because that's just the way it is," or "Because I told you so." It requires a degree of relaxation to want to respond to your child's inquiry with a question of your own. "Where do *you* think people go when they die?" "Why do *you* think people can't fly?" It takes time and patience to offer explanations as opposed to issuing edicts such as, "You can't go to the party because I said so."

It takes time and shared experiences to build a *close* relationship with your child. When your daughter's best friend rejects her, you can offer bromides: "Well, that's part of growing up," or "Don't worry, you'll find another best friend," or "You'll realize it was no big loss anyway." Or you can take the opportunity to help your daughter clarify and articulate her feelings. You can take the opportunity to show her how much you care about her and her feelings. You can take the opportunity to show her how important she is to you. You can attempt to fill temporarily the void created by the loss of someone whom your daughter loves.

But all of this requires time.

Your children need your wisdom. As a role model, you will teach them how to be in the world. You will provide a source of values. Your sons and daughters need you to provide them with a healthy image of a man—your son, so he can follow in your footsteps, and your daughter, so she will choose a good person for future romantic involvement. But all of your potential influence requires time to be effective.

Keeping Your Promises to Your Children

Children remember. My four-year-old caught me last week. I had gone off to a symposium the previous Sunday and had, therefore, missed our regular special time together. (Yes, sometimes I get my priorities messed up too.) Four days later, Sarah asked, "Could we have our special time today because we didn't have it last time when you had to go away?" Unfortunately, Thursday was a day full of appointments and teaching commitments which I could not alter. I had to say, "No, I just can't."

I had broken my promise of Sunday special time to Sarah. I had let her down. In a small, and, thankfully, reparable way, I had made Sarah feel that she wasn't important to me. Children remember, even when we assume (or hope) they have probably forgotten. Children remember what is important to them—and your attention is very important to them.

Keep in mind that your child learns a great deal from how you relate to her. She learns, for example, whether people can be trusted, whether people will find her worthy of their interest. You influence her perception of the world and her expectations of it. Most significantly, you influence how lovable she believes herself to be.

Avail yourself, therefore, of any opportunity to make her feel that she is important to you. If you are in the midst of a project when your child approaches and asks, "Daddy, would you play with me?" do not simply reply, "When I finish this," or "Later." Let your daughter know exactly when you will play with her. "This will take me one more hour. I'll meet you in your room at four o'clock." And if you can't play today or tomorrow, take out a calendar for your child and mark down a promised date. And be sure to keep your promise.

Your children need you. Don't be fooled, for example, by your adolescent's rebelliousness, stabs at independence, and psychological separation, or her seeming alienation from you and everything you might stand for. Her sense of identity is still tenuous. Her vulnerability to rejection is acute. She needs your strong guiding hand and a belief that she can always count on you should she stumble along the way.

Find More Time for Your Wife, As Well

You and your wife need special time as well. Your children deserve psychologically healthy and happy parents. And there are few elements in your life which affect your happiness as powerfully as the quality of your marriage. Most marriages, particularly those involving children, are on auto pilot. The great majority of interactions between husband and wife are instrumental. They revolve around role responsibilities—How did Bobby's dentist appointment go? Did you speak to the automobile mechanic about that funny noise in the engine? Can you drive Julie to soccer practice this Thursday? Can you stop off at the cleaners tomorrow? What did the insurance agent tell you? To which camp should we send Donna?

Think about the elements which produced excitement, intimacy, closeness, and passion when you first met your wife. At the beginning, of course, there was the physical attraction. But a sense of intimacy developed as a result of conversation and increasingly personal self-disclosure. Remember the nights you sat up together just talking? Remember how much you wanted to know about her? Remember how much you wanted the two of you to share your deepest feelings with one another? Remember how thoughtful you were about one another? Remember how you wanted to anticipate what would please the other? Remember how the relationship took center stage in your life and all else seemed like background? Those were the elements which forged the bond between you. And they all required time.

I am going to give you a gift, two gifts in fact. Within the next couple of weeks, I want you and your wife to have two romantic evenings. Let me explain. First, take out your respective calendars and decide which two evenings in the next two weeks would be free and unhurried. Each of you then choose one of those evenings to be "your evening." When it is your evening, you must assume *complete* responsibility for setting up that evening and choosing activities which you believe would be romantic for *both* of you.

If you can get the children to bed early or farm them out to various friends and relatives, the evening may consist of you or your wife making a candlelight dinner at home and preparing a special dessert to be eaten in front of the fireplace. Or it may begin with a walk on the beach at sunset, followed by dinner at a romantic restaurant on the coast. To reiterate, it can consist of whatever you believe would be romantic for the two of you.

When it is your evening, you are only to give your spouse three pieces of information ahead of time: where to be, what time to be there, and what to wear. And remember that when it is your evening, you must take complete responsibility for it. So, for example, if your evening includes your fixing a candlelight meal at home, you cannot say to your wife, "Honey, could you stop off on your way from the office and pick up a bottle of wine?"

A few more rules for these evenings: (1) Do not talk about "role responsibilities." Talk about each of you—your thoughts, your feelings, your dreams for the future, your fantasies, your hopes for your marriage. (2) While you are allowed to be as affectionate as you would like with one another during the evening, you are not allowed to have any sexual contact until the evening is over. (3) Be sure to choose evenings when you are not likely to be tired, stressed, preoccupied, or hurried. (4) Plan the situation beforehand so that there are no interruptions during the evenings.

The evenings are designed to give your marriage a likely needed booster shot of intimacy. They may also remind you of what has been missing in your relationship and why you have lost a sense of emotional closeness. Hopefully, they will spur you to set aside periodic times for these "lover" type interactions. Feeling more loving with your partner will inevitably spill over into feeling more loving toward your children.

Stealing Time

I know that you do not have a great deal of free time to spend with your children. You must, therefore, make the most of your possibilities. Running errands with your child can be quality time together—time to play word games, time to sing together, time to talk to one another. Turn the television off during dinner and do not allow your energies toward your child to be distracted by a battle over the consumption of his peas and carrots. Fathering is not just about being there for the milestones in your child's life. It is about being connected and attuned on an ongoing basis.

Are there any time-consuming activities which you inadvertently omitted from your list at the beginning of this chapter which could be eliminated by being better organized or by paying someone else to do them? From which of the activities on your list can you steal some time? Right now, choose three of those activities which are not family-oriented and force yourself to eliminate a total of at least ninety minutes a week from them.

Having asked hundreds of men to do this, I can assure you that the actual pain will be minimal. Remember, too, that when you are a happier person, when you are more enthused about life, you find that you need less sleep (which accounts for the greatest proportion of your time).

It would be unrealistic to expect that you will be able to make sudden, major changes in your life-style time allotments. Modifying your work life, for instance, may require some planning and preparation in order to implement a more efficient approach. But now, at least, you have a goal to focus on. And, hopefully, you can begin to make incremental adjustments to guarantee more quality time for your wife and your children. For now, try to spend one more hour a week with your wife and half an hour more a week with each of your children. I think you will observe an immediate enhancement of your feelings of closeness with each of them. And they will appreciate your statement of commitment and priorities.

The Larger Goal: Balance in Your Life

It sounds trite, but it's true: You need balance in your life. A balance between work and play. A balance between obligations you feel compelled to fulfill and activities which bring you joy. If you view spending time with your children as one more responsibility, as an additional chore, you will experience those interactions as "work." You must, therefore, learn how to enjoy your children in order to view them as a respite from the pressures of life. In order to truly feel that your children are a high priority, as opposed to intellectually knowing that they should occupy a treasured place in your life, you must do all you can to insure that your interactions are pleasurable ones.

Periodically assess whether your life reflects your priorities. Every three or four months, draw the three columns (Activities, Actual Hours, Ideal Hours) I introduced earlier and make your entries. In fact, let's check in now. Perhaps there have been changes as a result of reading the previous pages of this chapter.

ACTIVITY	ACTUAL HOURS	IDEAL HOURS

CHAPTER SIX

How to Discipline
with Love

Affection is not enough. Unconditional acceptance is not sufficient either. Your children crave guidelines. They require imposed limits for their sense of safety. Children are alarmed at their own impulses. They are frightened when there are no controls. And we are all apprehensive at the prospect of a capricious world, one which does not play by predictable rules. Laws and regulations still our feelings of vulnerability.

Children are born without control over their urges and without any understanding whatsoever of the necessity of self-control. They will learn how to control themselves from you; and your effectiveness in teaching discipline will greatly determine your child's future success in imposing mechanisms of self-regulation. Will your son be overly critical of himself, unforgiving, unable to feel comfortable with any gratification? Or will he be excessively self-indulgent to the point of self-destruction? Will he be able to find a middle ground which will provide a balanced sense of responsibility *and* self-satisfaction?

Will your daughter be able to tolerate frustration? Will she accept the fact that she cannot always have what her heart desires or will she feel forever deprived and resentful? Will she concede that others have urgent needs as well, needs which may not coincide with her own but which, nevertheless, must be respected? In other words, will she be able to relate to others in a loving, unselfish manner? Or will she fervently believe she deserves whatever she wants and, therefore, be unable to have a mature relationship?

You must also tackle the difficult task of discipline so that your child does not run your life or the life of your family. You must tackle the unpleasant task of discipline in order to insure that each member of your family gets his or her fair share. You must meet the challenge of being an effective disciplinarian in order to maintain your sanity.

Your son's and daughter's need for limit-setting never really abates. Your younger child needs to calm the anxiety generated by her deepest, unconscious desires. Your daughter's intense ties to her mother belie her not-so-obvious impulses toward you which threaten to overwhelm. "I want to marry daddy," she feels. "And I hate anyone else who is married to him," is the unconscious correlate.

Your teenager also craves your attention. Despite his struggle to separate from the nucleus of the family and establish an identity of his own, he still wishes to remain a part of it. He must be able to touch base, to feel confident that you care. And one fundamental way to demonstrate that you care is to go to the trouble of requiring regulation of his behavior.

Fifteen year old Jessica is typical of many teens I meet who are straining to move ahead with their lives more quickly than their age warrants. And then the real world reminds them of their vulnerabilities.

In her fashionably torn jeans, nails painted a bright red, Jessica presents a picture of someone who knows who she is and what she wants—except when she speaks with me in my office and her eyes betray a childlike tentativeness, a grappling uncertainty. "I went to a party with a couple of girlfriends last Saturday night," she recounted to me during a session. "We knew some of the kids, but there were a lot more who we didn't know, particularly some older guys. There was a lot of dancing and drinking and some drugs. I had a couple of beers and things started getting out of hand. There was a guy who I was dancing with . . . I think he was about eighteen or nineteen . . . and he was coming on to me really strong. I didn't want to seem like I couldn't handle it, but . . . my girlfriends had been drinking, too, and they were dancing in another part of the room. The guy started kissing me . . . and getting pushy. I was uncomfortable . . . He kept pushing . . . and I got scared. I ran over to my friends and told them we had to go right away."

Jessica was lucky. She got out just in time. But her behavior reflects the ambivalence and apprehension with which children explore their impulses and the world.

What Kind of Father Are You?

Like the other aspects of fatherhood that I have discussed, how you relate to discipline can give you an opportunity to discover more about yourself. It can also give you a chance to change and grow; to become the kind of parent—and person—you want to be.

Experts have described three types of parenting styles:

The *Authoritarian Father* is likely to produce fearful, anxious, depressed children. He

- is insensitive to the needs of his child

- prohibits disagreement between himself and his child

- maintains excessively tight controls

- is overly critical of his child

- rejects his child's suggestions out of hand

- always demonstrates impatience with his child

- is continuously judgmental of his child's performance.

The *Permissive Father* is likely to produce manipulative children who are unable to tolerate any frustration of their wishes. He

- fails to set adequate limits for his children

- rationalizes his abdication of his role as parent ("She's so cute. How could I refuse her?" "I didn't want to generate bad feelings between my son and me by saying, 'No.' " "It just became too much of a hassle to argue about it.")

- reflects his excessive need to be liked by his children.

The *Authoritative Father* is likely to produce confident, empathic human beings. He

- sets realistic and fair rules

- expresses warmth and affection without being unduly permissive

- admits his mistakes

- explains the reasons for his decisions

- clearly defines limits for his children

- is encouraging

- is not overly critical, belittling, or impatient

- adapts his expectations to his child's increasing abilities

- is sensitive to the singular needs of his child.

Which type best describes you?

Children trust fathers who are compassionate. Children admire fathers who are firm but fair. Children resent fathers who seem arbitrary and totalitarian. Children lose respect for fathers who fail to set limits, who abdicate their parental responsibilities.

Being both an effective disciplinarian and a loving father is a tremendously challenging but critical task. What kind of father do you want to be?

Strategies That Don't Work

Mr. Nice Guy

Some fathers find playing the role of disciplinarian extremely difficult.

> "I'm not going to be cruel to my children like my father was to me."
>
> "I want my child to have everything I didn't have."
>
> "I want my child to be happy, and if that will make him happy, I'm glad to give it to him."
>
> "I can't stand the whining and the tantrums. I would just as soon give it to her and not have to endure them anymore."
>
> "I don't have the energy to fight with my daughter. It's a lot easier to just say, 'Okay.' "
>
> "When it comes right down to it, it's not such a big deal anyway. Why not give it to them?"
>
> "It's not spoiling them. I just want them to be happy."

Note some of the problems with the above rationalizations.

"I'm not going to be cruel to my children like my father was to me."

You must be your own person. Not being like your father is not the basis for an effective parenting strategy. By simply reacting to the fathering you received, you are unable to address the real needs of your own children, especially their need for limits.

"I want my child to have everything I didn't have."

You cannot presently satisfy what *you* were previously denied. Giving your child everything you didn't have will not quell *your* childhood frustrations and resentments. Also, you assume that giving them everything you did not receive will make them happy. Perhaps their needs are different from your own when you were their age.

"I want my child to be happy, and if that will make him happy, I'm glad to give it to him."

You will not insure your child's happiness by giving him any one thing. Your child's happiness obviously depends on so many factors, some of which you control (e.g., your attention, your understanding, your support, your love) and many which you do not.

"I can't stand the whining and the tantrums. I would just as soon give it to her and not have to endure them anymore."

You must find the patience to discipline your child for her own good. When your child whines or throws a tantrum, you should simply tell her that you will not listen to her when she speaks that way. If she persists, you remove yourself from her presence. With no audience in sight, her behavior will lose its value. You cannot abdicate your responsibility as navigator of your family. You must not miss the opportunity to use your powerful influence to shape a psychologically healthy child.

"I don't have the energy to fight with my daughter. It's a lot easier to just say, 'Okay.' "

You can use the strategy of "Consequences," discussed beginning on page 106, to avoid fights. Also, if you have so little energy left for your children, it may be time, once again, to reassess your priorities.

"When it comes right down to it, it's not such a big deal anyway. Why not give it to them?"

It probably is not a big deal as an individual instance. But do not lose sight of some of the larger goals of discipline: to help your child accept the fact that he cannot have everything he wants and to teach your child that coping with frustration is an essential part of life.

"It's not spoiling them. I just want them to be happy."

We all want our children to be happy. But what are the best ways to increase the probability of their happiness?

One other common explanation I hear from fathers for their inability to be firm is, "I don't want my child to see me as a disciplinarian or a distant authority figure. I want him to see me as a friend." Oftentimes, however, these fathers are motivated by more than a desire to be a buddy to their child. These fathers fear losing the love of their children and, therefore, capitulate whenever they unconsciously anticipate that possibility. So they continually "bribe" their children by their assent. Unfortunately, unless the fear of rejection which these fathers harbor is resolved, it will forever dictate behavior which will not be in the best interests of their children.

One other potential difficulty with "giving in" or always wanting to please your child deserves mention. No child can stand to feel that a sibling is getting more than she. Capitulating to one child, therefore, will produce a chain reaction. ("You let Cindy get away with it, why are you being so mean to me?") Pretty soon, you will feel as though you have lost all control in your family. You will be giving more than you want and feeling uncomfortable about what you have allowed.

I Won't Be a Pushover

At the other end of the spectrum, some fathers approach discipline as a challenge to their manhood. They worry, "Am I being tough enough?" They resolve that they will emphatically demonstrate to their children who is boss. Suddenly, the argument or confrontation between this father and his child becomes a test of his will, his mettle, his power. ("I'm not going to let that snot push me around. I'll show him!")

Parents cannot afford the luxury of *acting* on their angry feelings toward their children. The function of discipline is to help the child. It is not to gratify the parent's impulses. The parent-child relationship is not the appropriate arena for a father to compensate for his feelings of inadequacy or express frustrations from another part of his life.

When you engage in a power struggle with your child ("Yes, you will!" "No, I won't!" or "If you don't do as I say, you're going to be in big trouble!" "I don't care!"), the issue which elicited your battle becomes obscured. The objective (i.e., behavior change) is lost as each side digs its heels in and becomes determined to "win." Fathers get caught up in commanding the respect of their child and trying to insure that they maintain control over situations. Children then feel compelled to assert their autonomy and independence. Now, your egos and the nature of your relationship are on the line. The skirmish has gotten completely out of hand.

One reason fathers and children overreact is because they hold grudges. "Maybe you got away with it last time, but I'll be damned if you will this time!" a father thinks. "You're always so unfair with me. I can't let you do that to me anymore," a child feels. Here, both father and child have their backs up because they retain old resentments. As we all know, old, unexpressed feelings contribute to present reactions being less than fair and rational.

Professional mediators always emphasize that both parties must (1) feel that their needs are understood by the other and (2) believe that the agreement which is reached is ultimately in their best interest. When parents always impose their will on their child, the child feels as though his desires are never being taken into consideration. When a child always gets his way, the parent winds up feeling impotent, inadequate, and unable to stand up for what he believes is right.

In any case, you will not win a war with your child. The fighting will simply escalate. And even if you suppress a child's unacceptable behavior at home, he has many other means at his disposal to express his anger and rebelliousness. You do not have control over his life when he is at school or out with his friends. Remember, the goal of discipline is not simply capitulation by your child. He must ultimately accept that the limitations you have imposed are just and fair.

The Problem with Punishment

We all want our children to feel happy, not sad. We all want our children to feel good about themselves, as opposed to guilt-ridden or self-critical. Yet so many fathers choose to discipline with punishment and not reward.

We punish because we are angry and wish a measure of satisfaction. We punish because we fear spoiling our children. We punish because we take our children's defiance personally. ("I'll show you who's boss!") We punish in order "to teach him a lesson." We punish because that is the way we were treated when we misbehaved or did not conform to the expectations of our parents.

Yet, for the most part, punishment does not work very well: *Punishment does not teach desirable behavior.*

You often feel guilty when you punish your child, especially if your level of frustration has prompted you to enact rather draconian measures.

When you frequently punish, you reinforce the sense of a battle between opponents. Your child sees you as the enemy.

As the astute child psychologist Haim Ginott has said, the problem with punishment is that it is a *distraction*. Instead of feeling sorry for what he has done and thinking about how he can make amends, the child becomes preoccupied with fantasies of revenge.

Finally, punishment loses its effectiveness as your child gets older.

Whenever I lecture to a parent group about discipline, a question about spanking inevitably arises. Is spanking a form of child abuse? Is spanking traumatic to the child? Is it *ever* okay to spank a child?

"My old man gave me the paddle sometimes when I deserved it. And I turned out okay," a father remarks. Oh, how easily we forget. At the time this father was paddled, I am quite sure that he did *not* feel as though he deserved it. On the contrary, he felt that his father was using his power arbitrarily. He felt that he was receiving cruel and inhuman punishment. And he felt awful because of his impotence.

Maybe this father did turn out okay. But my guess is that he grew up a highly self-critical individual who developed a habit of lashing out when he is frustrated. My guess is that this father has never learned how to really talk, reason, and negotiate with his child. I ask this father a rather funadmental question: *"Did the spanking you received from your father lead to greater closeness or greater distance between the two of you?"*

When my father hit me with his strap, I hated him. How weak and helpless I felt. After my father spanked me I *feared* him more. I did not love him more. And I certainly did not learn anything constructive for my future.

"I spanked Johnny because he was out of control," a father explains. But when this father spanked his son, it was *he* who was clearly out of control. Remember, a parent does not have the luxury of simply acting on his anger or frustration with his children.

A couple of other problems with spanking. As Haim Ginott reminds us, "Spanking relieves guilt too easily: the child, having paid for his misbehavior, feels free to repeat it." In addition, keep in mind that you are always a model of behavior for your child to imitate. The lesson you teach when you spank is: When you are angry, hit!

Strategies That Do Work

The Notion of Consequences

The word "discipline" conjures up such negative feelings, for when you were a child, you probably experienced it as punitive, excessive, irrational, and arbitrary. As adults, we often experience discipline or criticism by an employer or superior as humiliating. The word "disciplinarian" sounds even harsher. We imagine the ogre with the strap, the spinster teacher with her hair in a tight bun, menacingly tapping a rod into the palm of her hand.

But when you discipline appropriately, you are loving and teaching at the same time. When you discipline, you instill in your child a sense of responsibility because he learns there are *consequences* to his behavior. When you have clearly set out your expectations of your child and the consequences of his failure to meet those expectations, you have emphasized that your son or daughter is making active choices about his or her life. You, then, do not seem so arbitrary a taskmaster. You will be less frightening a figure to your child because you are predictable. Clear-cut cause and effect relationships are comforting because they can be anticipated. By emphasizing consequences, you will also implicitly be giving your child a greater sense of control over his future and preparing him for the real world.

"When you finish all of your homework, you can watch television."

"When you pick up all the clothes from the floor of your room, you can go over to Barbara's house."

"When you finish that entire glass of milk, you can have another cookie."

"If you play with your sister in your room for an hour so I can concentrate on my work, I'll take you for an ice cream cone."

Notice, that in all of the above examples, the expectations are made very clear and explicit at the outset. If you simply say to your child, "You can get that new bicycle you want when you start acting more responsibly," there is too much ambiguity. In what specific ways should he be more responsible? How do you define "responsible"? How does your child define "responsible"? How will you and he know exactly when he has acted responsibly enough to warrant the bicycle?

Not all quid pro quo consequences (i.e., If you do _____, then _____.) involve an interaction between you and your child. Every school morning, in millions of homes in America, low levels of pandemonium and high levels of parental anxiety reign. The Question always lingers in the air: "Will he be ready in time for school?" "Are you up?" "Have you finished dressing yet?" "Have you washed your face and brushed your teeth yet?" "Have you finished your cereal yet?" "Do you have all your books?" "Did you take your lunch box?" "Did you wear a warm enough jacket?"

You are constantly pushing and always worried. By the time your children are out the door, you are tired and irritated. And you haven't even started *your* day yet. What do you think would happen if you ceased your cajoling and your child were late for a few consecutive days?

Younger children need your assistance and reminders. But older children can learn that there are potentially harmful consequences when they act irresponsibly. If your ten-year-old forgets his lunch box occasionally, that is to be expected. But if he forgets it frequently, he must learn that you are not going to bail him out by bringing it to his classroom. Hunger is a powerful motivating force. You will observe that your son will soon be reminding himself to check for his lunch box when he walks out the front door if he faces the prospect of a grumbling stomach.

"Dinner is at six," you tell your eleven-year-old daughter.

"I'm not hungry," she replies.

"Okay, but that's when you can eat. I'm not serving anything later and you can't have any junk food if you get hungry."

"I don't care."

One hour later, after your daughter has finished her telephone conversation with her best friend:

"Dad, I'm hungry."

"Sorry, dinner was served an hour ago."

In each of these instances, you have taught your child about consequences. And just as importantly, you have spared yourself the anxiety and frustration inherent in nagging and reminding. You can relax a bit because the responsibility has clearly been shifted off of your shoulders and onto your child's. You can rest easier because you know that you have not been cruel or unfair. You have simply given your child reasonable choices.

In teaching your child about the notion of consequences, you must distinguish between feelings and action. It is okay for your son or daughter to express *any* feeling. In fact, the verbal expression of feelings can serve as a safety valve and prevent destructive behavior. And by your permission, you will be implicitly teaching your child about the importance of the direct expression of feelings for future, adult relationships. She can feel angry. She can tell you (or her brother, her sister, her mother, etc.) she is angry. But she cannot *act* on that anger. She cannot (1) physically harm another, (2) physically harm herself, or (3) destroy property.

If you and your child operate on the understanding that actions (or inactions) generate consequences, then you will also be able to avoid the following scene:

"Clean the mess on your desk."

"I don't want to."

"I said, 'Clean the mess on your desk.' "

"But, I didn't make the mess. Wendy [her sister] did."

"I don't care. Clean it up."

"I'll do it later. I promise."

"Do it now!"

"No!"

"CLEAN THE MESS ON YOUR DESK!"

"NO!"

She slams the door in your face.

"Don't you do that to me!"

"Just leave me alone!"

"Not until you clean your desk!"

Instead, a different dialogue will occur.

"You can go to Gloria's house when your desk is cleaned off."

"I don't want to clean my desk now."

"Okay. Just as long as you understand you can go to Gloria's house only when it's clean."

You walk away. End of discussion.

Your child can say "No," all she wants. But the bottom line is that she must do it. And if she doesn't, she understands that she will have to suffer the consequences. It's clear and it's clean. It's her choice.

Making Contracts with Your Child

Discipline strategies based on consequences should be modified as your children get older. Negotiated rewards and solutions should gradually replace dictated ones. Written contracts are one means of preventing misunderstandings and later arguments about the terms of the agreement. In a contract with your child, a specific cause-effect relationship is spelled out:

> You can watch television after you finish all of your homework.
> Once a month, you can invite a friend to sleep over if you make your bed every morning.
> I will take you to Disneyland on your birthday if you play games with your sister once a week for two hours.

Note several crucial elements when contracting with your child:

(1) The terms must be specific. It won't work if you require that your son "listen to his parents" or "be nicer to his sister." You will inevitably leave yourself open to argument about whether the conditions have been sufficiently met. "But, I *have* been nicer to my sister," he will protest.

(2) Phrase the contract in a positive manner. Avoid, "You can't speak to your friends on the telephone until you finish your homework." A positive spin ("You can speak to your friends on the telephone after you do your homework") is inherently motivating. It is more effective than a threat, which will only produce resentment because of its heavy-handedness ("Unless you finish your homework, you're not speaking to anyone on the telephone!")

(3) You must be sure that the contract is reasonable, i.e., that it can be fulfilled given the capacities of both parent and child.

(4) You must stick to the terms of the contract. If your child messes up in another area of his life, the contract is not to be voided.

(5) The younger the child, the more immediate the payoff must be. For children under the age of five, one day is probably the longest possible interval between action and reward. Teenagers, on the other hand, can wait months, particularly for a rather grand prize.

Other Strategies That Work

There are few elements of human behavior we can predict with certainty. But there are a few principles of human learning which are ironclad. One of these we refer to as the principle of *positive reinforcement:* When an action is followed by a reward or payoff, that behavior is likely to be repeated. You must, of course, know the inclinations of the individual you are attempting to influence. The payoff must match his particular preferences.

Rewards, however, may not be entirely sufficient to produce the desired behavior. Children (and adults, for that matter) need *encouragement.* When you are critical instead of encouraging, your child will think, "Dad never likes what I do anyway, so why try?" Children, especially young children, also need your support. When you tell your four-year-old to put all of his toys away, give him a hand so that he does not feel paralyzed and overwhelmed by the prospect of the task. Tackling it together can also transform the activity into another one of those ongoing bonding interactions, as opposed to it simply being experienced as an onerous project by your child. By aiding your child, you have also insured success for him, a further proof of his competence.

Your child's room looks like a tornado tore through it. You tell your child to straighten it up. After she exhausts her protests ("It's not so bad."), excuses (her sister made the mess not her), and bargaining positions ("I'll do it after this program is over."), she stomps off resignedly. An hour later she emerges from her room and resumes her post in front of the television set. You proceed to inspection. "You didn't finish straightening up your room! There are still some toys lying around!" you shout over your shoulder.

A more effective strategy, particularly with regards to encouraging future behavior, would be to *praise* the ninety percent of the task which your daughter successfully completed. "You did a great job. You just need to pick up those few toys and you'll be completely done." When you reward your child for the part she does correctly, you instill hope and confidence in her. A good place to practice this approach is when your child is learning a sport or a musical instrument or engaging in any activity which requires skill and practice. Because we want our children to improve, our tendency is to comment on mistakes and shortcomings. Try devoting more of your attention and feedback to what your child does right.

Encourage progress. Encourage *effort*. When we give our children a reward for getting "A's" in school or making the all-star team, we communicate an unhealthy message: You are as good as what you achieve. And if our children believe an "A" or the all-star team is beyond their grasp, they will simply give up. Encourage effort. Teach your children that the end product is less important than the process of trying their best.

Unfortunately, when your child is doing things right—when he obeys his parents' requests, when he does his homework diligently, when he is kind to his sibling, when the family routine is not disrupted—we all too often fail to acknowledge his behavior. We feel silly praising his efforts because that's the way he should behave. What's the big deal? But recognizing his positive activities will provide encouragement to continue. It will also balance the occasions on which you have been critical of him. Perhaps, most importantly, you will be indicating that you do not take him for granted (just as you would not like your efforts to simply be taken for granted).

Be generous with your rewards. Contracts ("If you do _____ then I will give you _____" or "If you do _____ you can _____") are fine. They teach responsibility. But unexpected treats can teach valuable lessons as well. "Elisa and Jane, you've been playing so nicely together, I'm going to take you for ice cream." Your spontaneity will also inject a lighter element into this entire business of discipline.

Compliance can also be achieved by depriving your child of what is valuable to him. (Again, any leverage will require a knowledge of your child's particular preferences.) Here, too, the concept of consequences can short-circuit long arguments, pleas to your conscience, and reasons why your request is so unfair. "If you don't do _____, then you can't _____." End of discussion. Obviously, if a reward system works for your child, better feelings will be generated in the relationship.

Time-out is a strategy which has gained increasing popularity in recent years. When your child acts in an unacceptable manner, you give him a "time-out," i.e., you punish by sending him to an isolated place. Time-out not only stops the undesirable behavior, it eliminates having to suffer the excuses ("But I only did it because _____"), lies ("My sister did it to me first"), and tantrums. One of the most common reasons time-out does not work for parents is that they send their child to his room for that period of time—a place which is filled with pleasurable activities! For time-out to be effective, the experience must be one of deprivation. Try, for example, a corner or the hallway instead.

Children are people, too. They are entitled to be treated fairly and reasonably. In response to your child's question, "Why do I have to?", you owe him more than the simple invocation of your authority. ("Because I told you so and I'm your father!") While an emphatic "No!" is sufficient for a toddler, the older your child becomes, the more *explanation* he deserves.

Adele Farber and Elaine Mazlish, in their book *How to Talk So Kids Will Listen and Listen So Kids Will Talk,* offer alternatives to the simple response, "No."

Give information:

"Can I go over to Jimmy's house to play?"

"Your cousin will be here in just five minutes."

Acknowledge feelings:

"I don't want to come home now."

"I know it's hard to leave when you're having a lot of fun. Maybe we can plan when you'll go over again."

Describe the problem:

"Dad, can you take me to the ball game Saturday?"

"I'd like to but I've got to finish this report by Monday. Let's look at the schedule and choose another date."

Throughout, I have been emphasizing the need to understand and appreciate your child's feelings. But you have feelings, too. And you have the right to verbally express them. Your child must learn that his feelings are not the only important ones around. Moreover, your child must understand that his behavior not only evokes consequences for him but *effects others as well*. And when you voice your feelings, you are, once again, *modeling appropriate behavior*. Just be sure that when you express your feelings, you avoid "you" statements ("Why do you have to be so irresponsible?" "Why do you have to be so mean to your little sister?") and utilize "I" statements. ("It makes me angry when you _____." "I get frightened when you _____.")

All children crave the attention of their parents. *Parental attention*, therefore, is extremely reinforcing, particularly if a child is used to receiving very little of it. Your child may use words designed to shock you (even when he may not know the actual meaning of the words). When you do not respond with the intensity your child anticipated, he will soon realize the futility of that avenue. His inappropriate behavior will cease.

It requires a great deal of conscious effort not to repeat the discipline habits of our own parents. But one which must be avoided is "guilt induction." ("Are you trying to give me a heart attack?" "Why do you make me worry so much about you?" "Why are you trying to hurt me?") When we instill guilt in another, we also sow the seeds of resentment. And ultimately, you want your child's behavior to be regulated by a firm, internalized sense of what is right and what is wrong and not by how it will affect you.

Though their egos often get caught up in the power struggle, most fathers have the best of intentions. They want to teach their children. They want their children to be better human beings. So they look for guiding principles, and one which they latch onto is the "principle of consistency." Fathers know that it is important not to give contradictory messages. They understand that learning the notion of consequences often requires repeated trials for their child.

But in their desire to be consistent and also not be seen as a pushover, fathers sometimes lose sight of the other side of the coin—the importance of *flexibility*. Rules should be modified in changed circumstances, as long as your child understands the singular reason for the modification. Your flexibility then becomes a special treat to be savored by him. "Yes, you can stay up later tonight because mom and dad are having a party." (Children hate to go to sleep when there is all this excitement going on in the house.) Life is not only about rules. It is about spontaneity and generosity as well.

Let the Discipline Fit the Child

No one approach to discipline is best for all children. No one approach to discipline is best for all parents. Children arrive with biological temperaments making them easier or more difficult to teach. Their changing ages necessitate changes in discipline strategies as well. Parents, too, arrive not only with their particular temperaments, but the baggage of the kinds of parenting which they received.

Some children require greater firmness. Others thrive when you give them more leeway. Some fathers need more orderly children. Others are more easygoing and can tolerate more spontaneity and uncertainty. In choosing methods of discipline, therefore, you must appreciate the needs of your particular child and come to peace with what you can tolerate.

In order to discipline appropriately and effectively, it is critical that you have realistic expectations. What should you reasonably expect from your ten-year-old daughter as opposed to your three-year-old daughter? What should you reasonably expect of your nine-year-old daughter as opposed to your eight-year-old son? What should you reasonably expect of your child who was born with a "difficult" temperament as opposed to your child who always seems to have a smile on her face?

When your toddler uses your living room couch as a coloring book, you must control your disgust, your anger, and your urge to lash out. You take away the crayons and clearly state that it is not okay to color on furniture. Nothing more. If your child is acting in an age-appropriate manner, it is you who must modify the unrealistic expectations which generate your displeasure and exasperation.

For example, you must *expect* to repeat lessons for younger children. (When a father reacts, "I thought I told you, 'No!' ", he perceives his child's behavior to be an act of defiance as opposed to a normal symptom of the poor impulse control of a three-year-old.)

If you have never taken a five-hour car ride with two young children in the back seat, you are probably in for a harrowing time. You can head off some of the inevitable sibling fighting, whining, complaints, endless irritating questions ("Are we almost there yet?" "When *will* we be there?"), and noise level by taking along games, books, coloring paraphernalia, and other activities in which your children can become engrossed. You can plan for numerous bathroom stops and slight side trips which might be fun for your children and break their monotony. It is up to you to try and make the journey an enjoyable one. For it is absolutely unrealistic to expect your children to sit patiently and calmly through such a prolonged, boring procedure. "Unless you keep quiet back there, I'm never going to take you on another trip again," is not only untrue (because you probably will take them on another extended trip) but also unfair. You have made a completely unreasonable demand on your youngsters.

We often do not give our children enough credit. We take their *exceptional* behavior for granted. My eight-year-old daughter, Rachel, has always displayed a maturity and competence beyond her years. Therefore, at times when she responds in an irrational, petty, childish manner, I find myself unduly irritated and disappointed, as I have forgotten that she is, indeed, only a young child.

But even when our expectations are age-appropriate, we sometimes overreact to our son's or daughter's childlike behavior. Your eight-year-old still insists on having a light on in her room when she goes to sleep. Your nine-year-old clings to his ragged teddy bear at bedtime. Your ten-year-old clutches her infant blanket as she goes about her after-school routines. And you want to shout, "Act your age! You're not a baby anymore!"

Why is it such a big deal for you? Probably because you envision that blanket or teddy bear as an appendage to your child when he or she is twenty-five. Probably, because you view this behavior as an indication of your failure as a parent.

There is no substitute for understanding the motivations of your child. After a two-year hiatus, at the age of four and one half, my daughter, Sarah, started to request her bottle. My impulse was to say, "No, you're too old for that." I saw her request as a sign of regression and immaturity. And, of course, I, therefore, saw myself as somewhat of a failure as a parent. But Sarah was simply reacting to the birth of her baby brother who received bottles (and attention and love) while being cradled by his mother or father. Once I reminded myself of this connection, I no longer experienced exasperation and dismay at her repeated entreaties. And I also knew that this, too, would pass.

Relax. Your daughter will not be clutching her infant blanket when she is twenty-five. Your adult son will not be attached to his teddy bear instead of a woman. Your child will not force his wife or her husband to sleep with a night light in the bedroom. Your children are holding on to these safety nets because they are soothing and not because of a desire to be perennial two-year-olds. In time, they will no longer require those supports.

Another lesson: Let the small stuff slide. When your eight-year-old son is banging his drums while you are trying to read and relax, you think, "He's just trying to irritate me!" And you may be right. Sometimes, children will act mischievously as a means of asserting their identity. At other times, they may raise their noise level in order to get your attention and/or prod a reaction. Your reflex may be to address any "infraction," as minor as it may be, because you fear the worst—"If I don't stop this kind of behavior now, there's no telling where it may end." Try to pick and choose what is important to discipline. You don't want your interactions with your child to be disproportionately unpleasant ones. Let the small stuff slide.

Being a better father requires a general understanding of the different stages of your child's development. You will have a clearer idea of their capacities at every age and the psychological passages and conflicts which they are probably experiencing. You will understand why the "terrible twos" are referred to in that manner and be relieved to know that this period will pass as well. You will be able to understand the provocative behavior of your teenager instead of simply reacting to it. One accessible, informative, and easy to read guide is *How to Parent*, by Dr. Fitzhugh Dodson.

The Importance of a United Front

When it comes to discipline, you and your wife must be on the same team. When parents are not united, children feel insecure. They sense that the foundation of their family is not a solid one. There are five key elements to effective, unified discipline:

(1) Your decisions about discipline (other than ones made suddenly, on the spot) should be made away from the children so they do not perceive the differences in your attitudes.

(2) The rules which you and your wife apply should be consistent.

(3) You must support one another, even if you do not necessarily agree with one another.

(4) You must not undermine one another. ("Dad, mom said I can't go over to Rhonda's house. She's so unfair. It would only be for a little while. Please, can I?")

(5) You must equally assume the task of disciplining. (Otherwise, your child will always appeal his case to the easier mark. One of you will become the Good Guy who is to be approached and one of you the Bad Guy who is to be avoided.)

Maintaining a united front is often difficult. One parent's discipline style may be more authoritarian than another's. "I didn't think it would hurt if I let her do it just this one time," your wife tells you. And, indeed, your wife may not have consciously intended to undermine your rules for your daughter. Perhaps your wife's unconscious needs to undo the strict upbringing she received and the resulting feelings of deprivation she experienced prompted her reaction. But when parents differ about approaches to discipline, marital conflict inevitably ensues.

Repeated and passionate differences about discipline strategies may reflect deep resentments in the marriage. "There she goes again," he thinks of his wife. "Do you always have to . . . ?" she accuses her husband. Suddenly, the problem and focus shift once again from the child to the marital relationship. In more dysfunctional families, we may see one parent purposefully acting more leniently toward a child in order to forge an alliance against the mate. Oftentimes, the consistently harsh parent is displacing his anger that he feels toward his wife (or toward his own parents) onto his children. Particularly when a father feels alienated from his children and, at the same time, perceives his children to have a very close relationship with their mother, lashing out at his son or daughter may partially satisfy his need to get back at his wife.

Children need to admire both of their parents. You don't want to put them in the position of choosing between the two of you. For their sake, you should want your children to love you and your wife equally. For their sake, you should want your children to know that you and your wife respect and support one another.

The Bottom Line

Disciplining your child will be easier and more effective if your child respects you. Your child will be more receptive to your guidelines if he knows you have *his* interests at heart and not simply your own. Your child will be more responsive to your wishes if he knows that your decisions are motivated by love and not merely convenience.

Understand that you will screw up occasionally. You will lose your cool. You will not always have the patience to "understand" your child and will, instead, simply react out of your own frustration. But hopefully, after you react, you will reflect more rationally on what has occurred. And you can make amends. For example, you will not lose face with your child by acknowledging, "I shouldn't have yelled at you. I'm sorry," or "I shouldn't have hit you. I lost control and I'm sorry." On the contrary, you will abort his seething resentment and be able to address whatever the issue is in a more helpful manner. Fortunately, children forgive and keep on loving.

CHAPTER SEVEN

Why You Will Love
Your Wife More

Men occupy more positions of recognized status and power than do women. They usually make more money than women, and money is, perhaps, our pre-eminent symbol of achievement and worth. One result of this state of affairs is that, deep down, the husband tends to believe that his sphere, his work is more important and more valuable than the one occupied by his wife, who is the mother of their children. This is true even if the wife has a job outside of the home because (1) she is probably earning less than her husband and (2) she is still expected by her husband to fulfill the bulk of parental responsibilities.

Ironically, what could be a more "powerful" role than one which asks mothers to nurture and shape our children, the future of our society? But just as men do not receive many nods of approbation for being good fathers, women do not receive social recognition for being good mothers. We simply presume that women will be caring, nurturing, competent mothers to their children. We do not reward or acknowledge them for that.

Many husbands prefer their spouse to be a full-time mom

rather than one who divides her time between career and family. Perhaps this traditional model was the one he was exposed to and, therefore, one with which he feels most comfortable. This is what he expected his family life would resemble. Perhaps he experienced the pain of perceiving that his mother was never there for him when he was a youngster and vowed to insure a more available mother for his children. Or, perhaps, he would feel threatened by having a wife who competed with him in the world outside of the home. Perhaps he feels more secure knowing that his partner remains within the circumscribed boundaries of her traditional role. If she strayed too far into a wider world, where might that "adventure" lead her? But whatever the reason, this father is pleased to see his partner directing her energies to her children and her husband.

What's She Doing While I'm Out Slaying Dragons?

On the other hand, a man may resent his spouse if she occupies the traditional role of housewife, because "she gets to do what she wants—to be with the kids," while he toils under the pressures of a job which gives him ulcers and heartburn. On particularly gruesome days, even though he may have previously voiced his *preference* that she stay home and be a full-time mom to their children, he is still apt to fall prey to thinking, She's enjoying herself with the kids while I have to endure this! The reality, of course, is quite different from the perceptions and appearances.

The traditional mom may also have had the blissful fantasy of spending a great deal of fun-filled time with her children, while building a close, mutually adoring relationship. The original fantasy, of course, did not include changing diarrhea diapers, wiping up vomit, endless chauffeuring, children who yell, "I hate you," whining, and a complete lack of consideration for her feelings and needs. The real job of mothering was not quite what she had anticipated (nor what you may imagine).

George Weiser, a thirty-six-year-old lawyer and father of two sons, ages four and two, was sitting in my office complaining about his wife, Elaine. Too fatigued for sex and too preoccupied with the children, "Elaine is never there for me," George grumbled. "What about *my* needs?" he wondered with exasperation.

He went on. "For the life of me, I don't understand it. She doesn't work—I know it's not politically correct to say she doesn't work because she doesn't have a job outside the home. But she doesn't work like *I* work. She doesn't have the same kinds of pressures that I have. . . . What does she do with her time? Why is she always so tired? And why is she so irritable all the time?"

George, like most fathers who are married to housewives, can't begin to understand just how hard his wife *is* working. Nor does he appreciate the stress and frustrations of spending most of one's life taking care of small sons and daughters. George has probably had the experience of being left alone for several hours to care for his children while his wife was off elsewhere. And if he is like most of us, he was thoroughly relieved when his wife reappeared. He felt worn out, at the end of his rope, and ready for a respite.

But George and other fathers forget how stressful it is to keep up a constant vigilance so that our two-year-old will not break his neck. We forget the exasperation when we suggest six different, reasonable items for our daughter's dinner and are met with, "I hate that." We forget how overwhelmed we felt when our son had an "accident" in his pants. (What should I clean first? Do I have to touch this stuff?) We forget how irritated we get at the noise level, the tantrums, the crying, the sibling bickering, and the insolence. And because we haven't tried it, we have no idea of how hard it is to put in a ten-hour shift with the kids, as opposed to a few hours at a time.

We also forget that, despite the stress and responsibilities of our job, we have adult-adult contact during the day. Housewives speak with children morning, noon, and night. We forget that, despite the aversive pressures, we often have something tangible—a finished project, a promotion, a paycheck—to point to as a result of our endeavors. If she's lucky, our housewife has a relatively clean house and relatively well-scrubbed children at the end of a day—in other words, nothing which can feed a sense of pride. We forget and, therefore, we are convinced that our jobs are more difficult, more arduous, more stressful than *simply* taking care of a couple of kids.

And because we forget, we are irritated with her when we walk in the front door and see the mess, hear her yelling at the children (Why is she so impatient with them? we judgmentally question), and are left in the midst of chaos as she calls over her shoulder, "You take care of them now. I need a break!"

An Exercise in Appreciation

Here is what you must do in order to gain greater respect and a deeper appreciation for your wife. Urge your wife to spend two days at a hotel or with a friend and assume complete responsibility for your children during that period of time. By "complete responsibility," I include, for example, not having your wife arrange any play dates for your children ahead of time, fix any precooked meals, or lay out your children's clothing in anticipation of various activities. You must be completely on your own in caring for your children during this exercise.

If you cannot (or will not) take on this task, at least try it for a briefer period. Eight or ten hours alone with your children might leave you with a more indelible memory of what it takes to do it all day, every day, and a subsequent appreciation of the toll it takes on your wife. Please don't simply nod your head in assent. Until you try this, you won't really understand.

Of course, if your wife does work, or is working part-time while the children are young, she has even greater demands on her time and energy. Most working mothers face a full day's worth of child care and household duties when they get home. In this case, the above exercise can be just as valuable. Try to come home after an exhausting day at the office to begin cooking meals, doing the laundry, helping with homework, and getting the children ready for bed and for the next morning. Believe me, you will feel more exhausted than you thought you could.

Let Her Know You Care

Ask the typical father what is most important to him and he will answer, "My children." And yet, he does not value his wife's role and her attendant activities involved in nurturing his children as much as he should.

You are pleased that your daughter takes ballet classes. She has become more graceful, more dexterous, and more beautiful. Who drives her to those lessons? Who bought her those ballet tights and shoes? Who combed her hair in a way which makes her eyes seem to sparkle? You are thrilled about your son doing so well on his little league baseball team. He has become more self-confident, more popular with his peers, and more enthusiastic about his life. Who makes sure that your son arrives on time to his practices? Who takes his teammates out for ice cream after the practices? Who makes sure that his uniform is clean so that he looks like a smaller version of a major league athlete?

"But I do acknowledge all that," you may insist. But the little voice inside you remarks, "Yeah, but we couldn't do all of this if I didn't bring home my paycheck every week." Your wife is the keeper of the thing that is most important to you in the entire world. Yet you probably do not appreciate or respect her caretaking efforts as much as you should.

The remedy is simple. Let her know how much you love her because of how well she cares for your children. Tell her, and then give her a big hug (in front of the kids is best). Do it today.

We all want to feel appreciated. In fact, one of the most common complaints heard in marriages is, "I wish he/she would appreciate me more." You, at least, are more likely than your wife to be recognized by your peers for your efforts. As I mentioned earlier, your wife's efforts at raising healthy, happy children are likely to be taken for granted. When you explicitly and publicly recognize her work, she will naturally feel reinforced and encouraged to keep it up.

Because your wife is the mother of your children, you have an additional incentive for loving her more. When you love her more, when you give her more, she will have more love and enthusiasm to give to your children. You want your wife to be as happy and as relaxed as she can be under the circumstances. Just as happier men make better fathers, happier women make for more energetic, patient, and loving mothers.

Breaking into the Family Circle

One obvious form of giving to your wife is to become more involved in assuming child-care responsibilities. Some fathers, however, see obstacles to their involvement, even when those obstacles are not real. Art Potter is a thirty-two-year-old electrician and a father of a seven-year-old daughter and four-year-old son. I first ran into Art at a school PTA meeting. His daughter and my daughter Rachel were in the same class. We would periodically meet at school functions and chat about our girls' class projects, field trips, or the state of today's educational system compared to the one we experienced. As is often the case, knowing that I was a psychologist, Art's remarks, at first fleeting, and then more detailed, became personal as he revealed his frustrations and unhappiness.

He and his wife, Darlene, married when they were both twenty-three. Art expressed his subsequent surprise and disappointment. "We don't seem to have much of a relationship anymore. All she seems to care about is the kids. . . . I think she's too involved with them. Before the kids came along, I thought we had a great relationship. We had a lot of fun together. We shared the same interests. Sex was great. But since they've arrived on the scene, she has become completely caught up with them. Our marriage has been dropped by the wayside." And eventually, Art spoke of the difficulty he experienced connecting with his children as well. "I always feel like I'm an outsider, like there's this closed circle of Darlene and the kids. Darlene is so close with John [his son] and Sheila [his daughter]. I can tell they would always rather be with her than with me. Sometimes, I feel like a stranger in my own family."

Art's perception reflects that of many fathers. He views his wife and children as a closed unit, one which excludes him. For his benefit, for Darlene's benefit, for the benefit of the marriage, and for the benefit of his children, Art must, however, break into this circle. He must break into this circle so that he can experience the joys of fatherhood. He must break into this circle in order to prevent his wife from smothering their children. He must break into this circle so that he and his wife can rediscover their love for each other. He must break into this circle because his children need a father as well as a mother.

Art must first tell his wife how he feels. "I feel excluded." "I don't feel needed." "I don't feel loved." Note that while he expresses his feelings, Art does not blame. He begins his statement with "I feel" and not "You make me feel." He must then explain what he wants. And he must extend his requests from the global to the specific. For example, after he states, "I want to have a closer relationship with you and the kids," it would be helpful if he could articulate the specific steps he would like them to take in order to bring that to fruition: "I would like to take the kids to the park sometimes without you." "The next time you go to the mall with the kids, I want to go with you." "I would like you to urge the kids to ask me for help when they need it, to ask me questions about their homework, or to tell me about the exciting things happening in their lives."

And while Art begins to establish a closer bond with his children, he can simultaneously renew his marriage. He must express his feelings about the widening gulf in their relationship: "I love you but I feel hurt and disappointed because I don't seem to be important to you anymore." And he must specify the measures he wants to implement in order to repair that gulf: "I want us to spend more time together, just the two of us. I want us to talk more. I want us to make love more. I want us to feel the connection we felt to one another before we had children."

Because you want your children to be as self-confident and emotionally healthy as they can be, you should want to have as loving a relationship as possible with your spouse. You must explicitly recognize her efforts and respect her achievements. The more you love your wife, the more likely she will love you. The more you love and appreciate your wife, the more she will be able to love your children as well.

CHAPTER EIGHT

Why Your Wife Will Love You More

As you probably know, you are not first in your wife's heart. If someone started shooting at your family, who do you think your wife would shield with her body? (No need to be taken aback. You, too, would instinctively shield your children.)

Your wife would throw herself over her children not simply because of their innocent vulnerability. She would cover them because they are a part of her. They came from deep inside her. The attachment, the sense of oneness, the desire to protect which your wife feels for her children is unmatched. Your wife loves you. But the profound and primal love she feels for her children is a love which a man will never fully comprehend nor experience.

When you love your wife, you want to nurture what is most important to her. In this fortuitous coincidence of priorities, your children are most important to both of you. And when you nurture your children without selfish, ulterior motives, she will feel truly loved by you—which will induce her to love you more.

Our Most Common Complaints

Husbands complain about sex, or the lack of it.

"We hardly ever do it anymore."
"She never seems to be really into it anymore."
"She just lays there."
"She doesn't initiate anymore."
"She just goes through the motions."
"She's never seductive like she was when we first met."
"She's put on weight and doesn't care how she looks."
"Sometimes I feel like she's doing me a favor."
"If it were simply up to her, we'd probably never have sex."
"Sex seems to be the last thing on her mind."
"She's always tired."

Husbands also long for the ongoing nurturing and deference their wife gave them before the children arrived. They miss the woman who, in days past, anticipated their needs and focused a considerable amount of energy in promoting their happiness and satisfaction.

Wives' complaints usually lay elsewhere.

"He doesn't talk to me anymore."
"He's not affectionate."
"He's not attentive."
"He's not thoughtful of me."
"He takes me for granted."
"He doesn't listen to me when we talk."
"He's always preoccupied."
"He'd rather spend time with his friends than with me."
"He doesn't like to cuddle anymore."
"He doesn't understand me or my feelings."
"Our relationship doesn't seem terribly important to him."

Not surprisingly, wives usually feel more dissatisfied about issues surrounding feelings, understanding, relating, intimacy, and closeness. And there is one plea commonly heard from wives but rarely heard from husbands: I wish he were more involved with the children. Indeed, this may be the most frequent complaint I have heard during my twenty years of practice from wives who have children.

It makes sense. If your children are the most important elements in your life, you are going to feel most sensitive about their care and most hurt if you perceive your husband to be neglecting them. And because mothers have such a profound sense of oneness with their children, it is understandable that they would take it so personally. *Loving me means loving my children*, she feels. *A man, therefore, who does not actively father will inevitably trigger his wife's resentment.*

Mothers Who Don't Fit the Mold

Most wives readily allow their husbands access to their children, but Marie, a thirty-one-year-old mother of two girls was different. "My mother was never around, and when she was, she was drunk," Marie told me. "She hated my father. He drank, too. They were both oblivious to me and my sister. They didn't show up to my graduations or even to things like school plays I was in. They always promised they would, but they never made it. For a long time, I wanted them to be interested in me, to be my mom and dad. But gradually, I gave up. It hurt too much. I vividly remember, as a teenager, I swore over and over that I would never do that to my children."

As we might have anticipated, Marie felt compelled to make up for the inadequate mothering which she received. She became a "supermom." Nothing was too much for her children. Marie was a whirlwind—driving them here and there, making sure they had lessons of some sort after school five days a week, dressing them in the best clothing, trying to anticipate their every need. Her husband, Anthony, resented her excessive involvement with the children.

He was bitter about something else as well. Marie had crowded him out of a relationship with his daughters. She subtly encouraged her daughters to favor time with her to the exclusion of Anthony. She justified her behavior with remarks designed to sound cute and benign—"Girls want to stick together." "We understand each other because we're all girls." Over the course of our discussions, it became increasingly clear that Marie felt she had to do it alone; that she had to be both the father and mother who had been denied to her. By identifying so closely with her own daughters, she was also attempting to satisfy the little girl who waited in vain for the appearance of her parents at her graduation. She would always be there for her daughters, thereby magically undoing the hurt created by the absences of her own mother and father.

Carla, a twenty-nine-year-old mother of a son and daughter, also jealously guarded her "turf." Carla grew up with a very critical mother, one who clearly competed with her, particularly during adolescence. Carla's mother, Cookie, was beautiful but terribly insecure. Not having finished high school, Cookie felt intellectually inadequate and relied on her good looks to get her through life. Cookie's harsh judgment of herself promoted unrealistic, exacting standards for Carla, ones she inevitably failed to meet. When Carla entered her teenage years and her awkward gangliness gave way to a rather attractive young woman, Cookie became threatened by Carla's youthful beauty, which she unfavorably compared to her aging, fading appearance. As a result, Cookie became even more severe in her stated opinions about Carla.

As we would predict, Carla emerged from this relationship as an adult with little self-confidence. Her singular hope, her singular source of self-esteem became her role as mother to her own children. Being a nurturing, loving mom and best friend to her children would finally allow her a sense of self-worth. But Carla's attempt to prove something to herself and undo past hurts also caused her to interfere with her husband's role as a father. After several months in treatment, she acknowledged that she kept her husband from establishing a close relationship with either child "because I can't bear the thought that someone else could do as good a job at parenting my children as I could."

There are some women like Carla and Marie who desperately need to parent alone. They are, thankfully, exceptions. Most mothers want to feel part of a family unit (i.e., mother, father, child), want to feel supported by their husbands, and want their children to have two parents.

A Father's Critical Role

Father involvement is critical both in its general and more specific impacts. Children who are actively loved and encouraged by their fathers are likely to become more loving, confident, future adults. Conversely, a father who is unavailable to his daughter may teach her that men are untrustworthy and cannot be counted on for emotional support and intimacy. She will be more suspicious of men and skeptical of their intentions. More basically, she will be less likely to know how to have a relationship with a man because this model for a male-female relationship was denied her.

We want our boys to grow up to be "men" and our girls to become "women." Therefore, while girls can retain a closeness and identification with their mothers throughout their lives, boys must break many of the psychological ties formed during their infancies. Sons must move away somewhat from their mothers and embrace a more masculine ideal. At the same time that they promote their sons' masculine nature, fathers also provide a convenient alternative for satisfying a boy's needs for closeness and security.

A healthy mother will encourage a father-son relationship in order to bolster her son's identification with his father and ease the process of distancing himself from her. In a way, the father-son relationship also serves as a vehicle of transition from the inseparable bond which the infant originally experienced toward his mother to the separate individual the child must ultimately become as an adult.

While the vast majority of children will welcome a father's attention, a few, however, voice a clear preference for spending time with their moms. If that is the case in your home, then arrange for your wife to be away from the house when your children will have some free time. Although you may begin by being your child's "second choice" of playmate, the more enjoyable the contact between you, the more your child will look forward to future opportunities for interaction. Remember that your children want to be with someone who makes them feel good about themselves, who makes them laugh, who listens to them, and who understands them. Fathers can do all of that as well as mothers can.

Remember, too, that the quality of the encounters between father and child will be different than those experienced by the child with her mother. Your interactions with your child, therefore, will not supplant the need your child has for her mother, nor will it threaten your wife's special place in your child's heart.

Being a Better Father Will Improve Your Sex Life

For most women, love and sex are inextricably intertwined. This is particularly true in a long-term relationship. Sexual excitement is very much a function of the strength of her loving feelings for her man and her perception of his love for her. Here are some typical responses to the men's complaints from the beginning of this chapter:

"If you loved me more, I would feel more passionate."

"If you were more considerate of me, I'd be more interested in sex."

"If you were more affectionate, I might feel like making love more often."

"If you were more thoughtful, our relationship would feel more romantic to me."

You may want to have sex because of a certain buildup of sexual drive. You may want to have sex because your wife looks particularly attractive tonight. You may want to have sex because you feel generally tense. You may want to have sex because, earlier in the day, you saw someone or imagined someone who aroused you.

Your wife, however, wants to have sex when she knows you care. Your wife wants to have sex when she senses your love.

What does your wife treasure most? Her children. So when you are more involved with your children, your wife will love you more for that. And when your wife loves you more, she will want to make more passionate love to you. *There is no more powerful aphrodisiac to a mother than to see her husband lovingly engaged with their children.*

Heidi Slater, a petite, thirty-two-year-old substitute elementary school teacher, and her husband, Paul, a thirty-four-year-old mutual fund manager, had been married for eight years when they appeared at my office. Heidi and Paul had two children, a six-year-old son and a four-year-old daughter. Both Heidi and Paul were feeling as though they "were drifting apart." Sex was just one problematic area of their relationship. During our third session together, Heidi described a key barrier to her sexual desire. Her remarks underscored the inseparable identification which many mothers have with their children.

"Most of the time, Paul's simply distracted, not at all involved with the family. I don't feel that he's connected to me or the children. When he does interact with the kids, and I can tell he is truly into it, I feel completely differently toward him. I feel like he really cares about us. I feel closer to him. And I'm much more likely to feel like making love to him."

When your wife sees your involvement with her children, she will want to see you happy. She will, therefore, want to satisfy your sexual desires. She will be more likely to suggest that just the two of you get away for a night or a weekend so that you can have more intimate time together. She will be more open to sexual experimentation. She will be more sexually creative. She will take pains to make sure the children are tucked away early in the evening so that you can have uninterrupted time together. And, of course, when your wife is happier, her own libido is more likely to assert itself.

Supporting Her Career Desires

Even after the liberation movements of the 1960s and 1970s, it is the exceptional husband who fully supports his wife's career ambitions. We have been socialized to believe that men must develop careers and financially provide, while women bear babies and care for the hearth. When a woman plants a significant portion of her identity in the professional world, we often assume that she is "out to prove something." We view her as an aberration, a female who has abdicated her "natural" role of motherhood. Perhaps she's one of those angry feminists with a chip on her shoulder, we surmise. We test her sincerity and commitment. We look for signs of "softness." Instead of respecting women who achieve a great deal and rise to prominence outside of the home, we question what *drives* them. What are they trying to compensate for?

When a two-career couple must relocate to another city, that decision is usually determined by a deference to his career ambitions. We assume that professional achievements are more significant to a man's sense of accomplishment than to a woman's. He probably makes more money than she does, which also becomes a primary rationale for following his path of professional development. But should money be the only indicator of one's value or the reason for supporting one's creative expression?

As a husband and father, you should want your wife and the mother of your children to be as happy and fulfilled as she can be. You must, therefore, support the career aspirations which she may harbor. You must fight your tendency to assume that work outside the home is necessarily more important for male than for female fulfillment. Perhaps, most importantly, you must support your wife's *choice* of what she wishes to do with her life and respect her work, whether it is inside or outside of the home. You must also transform your self-image as a "secondary parent" into a more central one in order to enable her freedom to choose.

Sharing Household Responsibilities

Millions of women work outside of the home not necessarily because they have career aspirations, but in order to make ends meet. Their husbands' salaries are simply no longer sufficient to support families in a middle class life-style. Many of these husbands deeply regret this situation and wish that their wives could be full-time mothers if they wanted to. These men often burden themselves with unnecessary feelings of guilt and inadequacy because of their shortcomings as providers.

But whether it be out of necessity or choice, study after study indicates that when both husband and wife work full time outside of the home, the wife is still held far more responsible for child care and household duties than her mate. Children and home are her province, her responsibility, he has learned. She has been taught the same lessons, and so most women grudgingly accept this twofold burden. But even in cases where she has incorporated traditional socialized expectations so that she accepts this "double duty," she will feel overworked and underappreciated—feelings with which you can readily identify.

Other women, however, rail against these assumptions, as well they should.

Because they have been socialized to do whatever it takes to succeed and provide for their families, most men do not complain about their disappointments, frustrations, or pressures at work. "You do what you have to do," is their attitude. Similarly, women who accept their prescribed role as housekeepers do not grumble about cleaning toilet bowls, washing dirty underwear, or changing diapers. *But that doesn't mean they enjoy it.* Because our wives don't moan about it, we assume that they don't mind doing it, even while we are well aware of how unpleasant these tasks would be for us.

When your baby wakes up in the middle of the night, who gets up to check on him? Probably your wife. When your child gets sick, do you simply take care of her or do you immediately call your wife into the picture? If you are like most fathers, you probably follow the latter course. When it comes to parenting, particularly at times of trouble or crisis in their children's lives, most fathers see themselves as *helpers* and not coparents.

For many fathers, becoming more involved with child care and housekeeping may require cutting back on the hours they spend at work. This huge psychological step requires the un-equivocal support of one's spouse. She must help you feel secure enough as a man to give up some of the potential "male rewards" inherent in promotions and bigger paychecks.

Many wives lament the absence of their husbands: "I wish he were home more." "I wish he wasn't so tired and preoccupied all the time." However, they also expect to retain certain standards of living. But they can't have their cake and eat it, too. Having you more involved as a father and housekeeper will necessitate changes in attitudes and expectations for both you and your wife.

The birth of my first daughter helped sweep away my last vestiges of sexism. On repeated occasions, while observing some human achievement, I thought to myself, "If Rachel wants to do that, she should be allowed to." I want Rachel and my younger daughter, Sarah, to be whomever they want to be.

But they may require the support and encouragement of their future spouses to realize their dreams. And here's where you come in. By sharing household responsibilities, you nourish the worldly ambitions which your wife may cherish. Your wife can then become the role model you want for your daughters—a woman who can pursue her aspirations. Seeing you washing dishes, preparing meals, or doing the laundry will also increase the likelihood that your daughter will choose a husband who also sees these as his responsibilities, thereby freeing her for pursuits outside of the home.

Your sons also need to observe you acting as a partner in household chores. These observations will teach them to have more equitable gender expectations. They will become more loving husbands, encouraging their wives to exercise their full human potential.

You don't have to be bound by the traditional expectations and restrictions your father or grandfather may have placed on his wife. You can design your own roles and responsibilities within the family and support your wife in her interests and aspirations. When she knows that you want her to be all that she can be, she will love you more for that. And when your daughters identify with their mother and incorporate that image of limitless potential, they will feel forever grateful that you helped pave the way for their success.

CHAPTER NINE

The Marriage-Child Link

You can learn "fathering skills." You can have the best of intentions of being a good father. But unless you are *motivated* to become actively involved with your children, you will probably remain, for the most part, on the outside looking in. You will continue your immersion in your work world or justify your lack of family involvement with the belief that "mothers should bring up the children." You will remain a bystander who periodically assumes the trappings of fatherhood by taking your child to a ball game or to the circus. You will absent yourself from ongoing fathering because other aspects of your life retain higher priorities.

So where will the motivation to take a more active role come from? It may be born of your own childhood experiences. Those of us who, while growing up, enjoyed the benefits of a loving, involved father-son relationship may want to duplicate that experience for our children. Those of us who felt keenly deprived or even abused by our own fathers may be determined to provide an entirely different experience for our sons and daughters. But the most powerful and healthy source of motivation may be found in your present as opposed to your past. For study after study clearly indicates that *fathers who are happy in their marriages are more likely to be involved with their children and more likely to enjoy that involvement.*

Qualities of a Successful Marriage

What does a successful marriage look like? What does it feel like to each spouse? Distilled from the voluminous research about these questions, my twenty years of clinical practice with couples, and my own ten-year experience with my wife, here is a partial list of critical ingredients:

Spouses listen to one another. They care about the other, so they care about what the other is saying. They are attentive and interested. They display a high level of empathy for their partner.

Spouses are supportive of one another. They are there for the other during times of emotional duress. When their spouse is feeling badly, they provide comfort and encourage him/her to talk about his/her feelings. When necessary, they are willing to interrupt the flow of their lives in order to provide emotional sustenance for the other.

Spouses are emotionally open and intimate with one another. There is a mutuality of self-disclosure about fears, insecurities, and vulnerabilities, as well as hopes and dreams. It does not bode well for a marriage if there is a significant discrepancy in the willingness or ability of the two spouses to be open about who they really are.

Spouses resolve conflict constructively. During times of disagreement, neither spouse wants to win at the expense of the other. Instead, both partners strive for a win-win outcome, one which allows for mutual, partial gratification. These spouses negotiate instead of threaten. Although they are able to assert and articulate their needs, when they choose to accommodate the desires of the other and deny some of their own, they do not feel like they have "lost." They seek consensus instead of brandishing ultimatums. They work toward a resolution which does not leave the other with bitterness and resentment. They want their partner to be happy because they know that they will be traveling the same path together for a long time into the future.

Several years ago, a couple in their early twenties who had been dating for three years came to see me because they were unsure about whether or not they should marry . At one point, they both chimed in, "We have a lot of fun together." And in the next moment, "We *never* argue!" "Then you haven't really tested your relationship, have you?" I suggested. The proof of a relationship is not whether two people can get along or have fun together. The proof of a relationship lies in the couple's ability to constructively resolve conflict, for conflict in marriage is inevitable.

Resolving conflict successfully is always reassuring, for it is a statement of individual maturity and love for one another. When we see our partner's willingness to consider our needs, we often soften our own position because we are grateful for their consideration. We become more flexible because we no longer feel locked in battle but, rather, engaged in a cooperative effort.

Spouses encourage each other's growth. Husband and wife want the other to be all they can be. They encourage the other to become more aware of his or her strengths and actualize them. They are not threatened by change in the other, even though the equilibrium of the relationship may be temporarily disrupted by those changes. Nor do they place obstacles in the path of the other. Conversely, when a marriage is already an unsatisfying one, accommodations to one's partner and any resulting self-denial are resented.

Spouses trust one another. They trust the other's fidelity to the relationship. They stem any potential insecurities in the other by offering reassurance. Their singular commitment and attentiveness to the marriage inspires a quiet confidence in the other. Spouses also trust that the other will have their best interests at heart whenever decisions affecting them are made.

Spouses tolerate the expression of anger by the other. Upon hearing the anger of the other, spouses do not withdraw or eventually retaliate. They understand that the verbal expression of anger is vital so that the hurt feelings underlying the anger can be addressed. They understand that resentment must be expressed as soon as possible so that it can be dealt with, resolved, and moved beyond.

Spouses operate in the present. They are not driven by past hurts incurred during the marriage or in previous relationships (including those involving one's parents.) They are neither trying to undo previous slights nor compensate for previous frustrations. They react to present circumstances instead of allowing the evocation of old resentments to cloud their judgments and responses.

Spouses view marriage as a cooperative partnership. Spouses do not compete, they cooperate. They have no need to prove their superiority over the other. They do not exult in "having been proven right." They do not compete for the affection of their children. On the contrary, they foster their child's respect for their spouse. They are not fixated on defining what is "mine," and are more likely to think "our."

Spouses have mutual respect for one another. Husband and wife *act* respectfully toward one another. And they do not take each other (or the efforts of the other) for granted.

Spouses have a mutually satisfying sexual relationship. The bed is not the battleground where resentments are played out. Spouses are assertive about their sexual needs and responsive to the needs of the other. They are attracted to one another and are both willing to initiate sex in order to demonstrate their interest. They need not have frequent sexual contact if the sexual drive of both is low, but they are *affectionate* with one another in an ongoing way. Their love has an important physical component.

Spouses have similar role expectations. They are clear with one another about their role expectations, especially during times of family crisis or transition (e.g., the arrival of a child). They also have similar standards of performance for those roles (e.g., How clean must the house be? How much money should the breadwinner make? How involved should a father be with his children?).

Spouses have made a commitment for life. Their commitment to one another allows them to take a long-term view. Both spouses understand that their marriage may have prolonged periods of relative satisfaction and dissatisfaction. But even during periods of dissatisfaction, they do not have one foot out the door. *They are not continually monitoring their alternatives.* Rather, they invest the necessary energy in attempts to make adjustments in their expectations and/or in the relationship.

Spouses accept their spouse's shortcomings. While they may each have a wish for their ideal partner, they understand that no one is perfect. They have learned that there is no one out there who would provide the absolute "fit" for their interests, needs, and desires. They are not hypercritical of one another. On the contrary, they appreciate the fact that all of us come to a relationship with insecurities and inadequacies, and they empathize with those imperfections.

Spouses have realistic expectations of marriage. They know that "storybook marriages" are just that—stories, fiction. They are able to make favorable comparisons of their marriage to others with which they come in contact.

Spouses share decision-making powers. While spouses may appropriate certain domains because of their inclinations or expertise, both partners retain a perception of an equitable distribution of power in the relationship.

Spouses share similar values. Not only are spouses compatible companions for one another as they share similar interests, but they also possess similar, convergent values about what is really important in life.

Spouses act lovingly toward one another. These spouses understand that it is not sufficient to feel love toward one's mate. They *demonstrate* that love in a myriad of ways, thus further insuring that each feels loved by the other.

Spouses are able to apologize. Indeed, love entails the willingness to say, "I am sorry." Apologies are not viewed as concessions or indicators of defeat. Apologies come from love and sincere regret about having hurt the other.

Spouses maintain a "twoness" while forging a "oneness." Spouses are able to assert their individuality while making a profound commitment to the partnership of marriage. Neither partner feels threatened by the other's individual needs and desires because they have confidence in the strength of the commitment they have made to one another.

This list of indicators of a successful marriage is, by no means, an all-inconclusive one. (Nor does the list address the many functions of marriage which generate individual fulfillment. For example, one of the most vital effects of marriage is that it provides a sense of meaning to one's life.) Furthermore, our individual needs and the ongoing dynamics of the relationship will dictate the relative importance of each item to the success of the partnership. Factors will also ascend or descend in importance depending on the stage of the relationship and particular circumstances or crisis affecting it.

We all approach marriage with our unique sets of expectations. Some of those expectations will be realistic and others will not (e.g. that the relationship will continue as it was before the birth of a child). Some of those expectations will be fulfilled by our spouse, and others will remain unmet. One of our primary tasks in marriage is to be able to cope effectively with our inevitable frustrations and disappointments and focus on the rewarding aspects of the relationship.

It's easier, of course, to live up to this ideal description of marriage when life is going smoothly, when we are relaxed, and when we feel secure. Your extended family can provide invaluable, ongoing support. Household help can provide "breathing room" and can ease the potential strains that life imposes on a marriage. But every marriage faces unexpectable obstacles. People lose jobs or experience financial setbacks. Loved ones become sick or die. We find that we must uproot ourselves geographically. The resilience of every marriage will be repeatedly tested.

How Marital Frustrations Affect Our Children

Marital dissatisfactions inexorably spill over onto the children. Whether individual frustrations explode in the open or are kept inside, children are ultimately affected by their parents' unhappiness. Some family therapists have gone so far as to *assume* that all behavioral problems manifested by children result from marital discord.

A father may withdraw from family life because his relationship with his wife has become too painful or unsatisfying. Knowing how important the children are to their mother, the father may avoid or lash out at them as a means of punishing his spouse. Or he may taunt his wife by giving his children the affection which he withholds from her. Unfortunately, parents are apt to make the most critical, destructive remarks to their children when they feel deprived and angry: "You'll never amount to anything!"

When parents compete for the loyalty, affection, sympathy, and support of their sons and daughters, they often attempt to forge an alliance with their children against their spouse. A struggle for power in the marriage may lead one partner to contradict or undermine the other in front of the children. Parents may explicitly or implicitly force their child to "choose" whose side he is on. In choosing, the child inevitably loses, for pleasing one parent triggers a rejection by the other. Tragically, it is often the most vulnerable (i.e., most needy) child who is seduced into an alliance with a parent. This child's insecurities leave him most susceptible to manipulation and subtle threats of rejection. ("If you don't side with me, then . . .")

When the parents don't respect each other, each fears that their child will grow up behaving like the other. Because of their inability to control their fury, these parents make disparaging remarks which undermine the worth of their spouse in their children's eyes. Mother and father lose sight of the fact that children need to love and respect both parents.

Undermining a spouse is not the same as having a difference of opinion. Nor do they necessarily have the same impact on your children. When we undermine our spouses, we not only call into question their judgment, but we implicitly question the legitimacy of their role as parents. We encourage our children to disregard their advice or direction.

It may, in fact, be healthy for your child to observe you and your spouse having differences of opinion or even arguments, if they do not escalate into personal attacks ("The reason you believe that is simply because you're ignorant") and are resolved in a way that makes it clear that your relationship is stronger than your disagreements. It is reassuring for a child to learn that disagreement between mates does not necessarily lead to harm of one or the other parent, or the self, nor to a crumbling of the relationship.

We have already seen how some parents try to compensate for their own childhood deprivations by becoming overly involved with their children. Their conscious intention may seem to be a noble one—"to be the best parent I can be." But their excessive need for attention, validation, and a sense of accomplishment as mothers or fathers invariably causes them to neglect their marriages. And because they so desperately need the approval of their children, they avoid some of the necessary responsibilities of a parent—such as discipline.

There are many homes in which too much time and energy is directed toward sons and daughters at the expense of the marriage. In these cases, clearer boundaries often need to be set between the marital unit and the children. Spouses must understand that, ultimately, their children will benefit from a strong relationship between their parents. Often, a spouse simply needs a nudge to realize that her marriage is being taken for granted instead of getting the attention it deserves.

At times, a parental focus on a "problem child" may serve as a distraction from marital difficulties or as a convenient means of avoiding having to acknowledge those issues. Children want to squash parental wrangling as well. Over the years, I have often seen boys and girls actually develop physical or behavioral symptoms in order to purposefully divert their parents' attention from their marital conflicts. When parents fight, the specter of the possible dissolution of the family is raised in children's eyes. They may then go to great lengths to keep their family intact if they perceive its unity to be threatened, even offering themselves as sacrificial lambs.

Your children are not here to fill the void left by marital dissatisfaction and disengagement. They are not to be utilized as a substitute for adult-adult intimacy. They are not in this world in order to satisfy a wife's or a husband's need for love, closeness, or a sense of worth. A child's task is to fully develop his/her emerging self. When we place our children in the position of satisfying our needs, we rob them of their childhoods.

You owe it to your children to have a satisfying marriage. If you and your wife do not have that kind of relationship, you owe it to yourselves and to them to seek professional help.

Placing the Blame Where It Doesn't Belong

After twenty years of practice, I've probably heard everything. One comment I have heard too frequently (mostly from men), however, is, "Until the kids came along, our marriage was fine." Usually, that assessment is simply not accurate. For, with few exceptions, children make a good marriage better and a poor marriage worse. The presence of new responsibilities strains an already tenuous bond. More accurate and honest statements by these men might have included:

> "I needed my wife's attention so much that I could not tolerate a rival for that attention."
> "Our marriage was good enough to cover our dissatisfaction with one another. But when our child arrived, it placed demands on us and created further deprivations in the relationship which caused other frustrations to surface."
> "My wife was never very affectionate or loving, but I

assumed that it was just the way she was. Then we had a child and this whole, other, warm, caring side emerged. I resented it. Why hadn't she been that way with me?"

"We never really had a great marriage, but I still felt we had something of a relationship. When our child was born, my wife turned all of her attention to him."

These fathers are angry. They had not anticipated the significant marital changes which would occur when their child arrived on the scene. When they first married, they assumed that she, they, and the relationship would, for the most part, be that way for the rest of their life. These fathers were blindsided by the transformations.

But a reasonable man can't *blame* his wife for loving their child. Instead, he may become impatient with his son or daughter. In his mind, his child has now become the source (or, at least, the compounder) of his dissatisfaction. However, instead of addressing his marital frustrations with his wife, he victimizes the child.

When their children develop problems, these husbands, consciously or otherwise, frequently blame their wives. Because she is the primary caretaker, she is held responsible. If the problem persists and his tension and dissatisfaction escalates, he will become increasingly judgmental. What did you do to make our child be this way? he silently accuses. Why can't you take care of this problem? he impatiently wonders. Now, not only is his marriage an ongoing personal disappointment (for which he blames the children), but his children are adding to his misery (for which he blames his wife).

Perhaps a word of caution about blaming *yourself* is in order here. With our increasing awareness of the importance of socialization and parenting in the emotional life of our children, many mothers and fathers have taken on more personal responsibility for their children's problems than is warranted. They are too critical of their efforts and too quick to find the causes of their sons' or daughters' problems in their own inadequacies. Empirical findings seem to indicate that genetics and inborn temperament play a much greater role than we had appreciated in determining problematic behavior. In any case, your guilt helps no one. In most cases, guilt only paralyzes. Direct that energy instead toward concrete steps which may alleviate your child's distress.

Why Your Children Need to Observe a Healthy Marriage

When a child is pulled into an alliance with a parent, he is deprived of his right to a mother *and* father. When a child is mired in the adult maelstrom of martial conflict, he is cheated out of his innocent, carefree years.

Perhaps you grew up witnessing relentless marital discord. It probably frightened you. Parents are supposed to anchor our world and provide the stability we need to calm our normal childhood anxieties. Instead, you may have viewed your parents' conflicts as the first steps toward family dissolution and, perhaps, abandonment. For a child sees the world through inexperienced eyes. He thinks concretely. When a spouse says to the other, "I can't take you anymore," a youngster will imagine a foreboding finality. He has not yet learned that what we say in anger is seldom realized.

Some children insert themselves between their warring mother and father in hopes of quelling the storm. Other children close their bedroom doors and shut out the acrimony as a means of reducing their anxiety and sense of vulnerability. But whatever the immediate reaction to parental hostility, children will later emerge wary of intimacy and the opposite sex.

Instead of observing a marriage whose wounds were periodically exposed by battling partners, you may have grown up in a home where husband and wife had *emotionally* withdrawn from one another while remaining a functional unit. They had already given up any hope for personal satisfaction in the marriage and perhaps remained together "for the children." The atmosphere was probably a depressed one, devoid of warmth, affection, or humor. The people you cared about most in the world were profoundly unhappy, and you knew it.

Healthy marriages can respond more constructively to the challenges and crises of parenthood. The absence of warm, caring feelings between spouses in an "emotionally withdrawn" marriage lessens that possibility. In these families, spouses, absent a sense of partnership, will not be able to count on each other's emotional support in dealing with difficult issues. They'll lack the desire to share burdens and responsibilities, and their frustrations will cloud their abilities to make decisions in the best interests of the child. They will often lapse into blaming one another instead of facing problems which require them to focus on their child's insecurities and conflicts.

The end of childhood must culminate in a son's or daughter's separation from their parents and from the nuclear family. Healthy parents encourage this process. A loving, close marriage implicitly creates clear boundaries between parents and child which can ease this movement away. The alliances and dependencies that spring from marital dissatisfaction, on the other hand, cause mother and father to retain a pull on the child. Unfortunately, many children feel obliged to curb their own independence in order to neutralize a parent's melancholy or maintain a precarious marital accommodation. Research indicates that children who forsake their own best interests and remain bound to their parents will develop greater psychological difficulties later on than will their siblings who escaped this debilitating environment.

Children are continually observing how mother and father (the prototype of Woman and Man) treat one another. Does their manner of relating engender fear or wariness or anger in the child toward the opposite sex and impair future intimate relationships? Or do the child's observations of the parents' marriage lead to expectations of warmth, support, caring, and closeness? Do mother and father treat each other with respect or with disdain?

There are no perfect marriages, and most children can live with that knowledge. But your children will not thrive if they are continuously exposed to marital frustrations and seething resentments. *You owe it to your children to make your marriage the best that it can be.*

CHAPTER TEN

Divorced Dads

It happens one million times a year in America. But no matter how commonplace it may be, divorce is heart-wrenching for every father, mother, and child involved in its process.

Divorce is a decision filled with uncertainty. Uncertainty about its correctness (How bad does the marriage have to get before I call it quits? How badly do I have to feel before I leave?) and uncertainty about the future (What will this do to my life? Can I survive going it alone? What will it do to the children? How will they fare in a broken home?). Oftentimes, estranged spouses do not anticipate the extent of their feelings of loss and loneliness as they more urgently focus on the anticipated relief from their difficult situation.

Mothers and fathers will feel guilty about destabilizing their children's worlds. And despite the almost normative nature of the event, husband and wife will feel as though they have failed. We read that there is no longer any social stigma attached to being a divorcé in the 1990s. But husband and wife often feel ashamed nonetheless. Our marriage, with its attendant hopes and dreams, began so brightly. How could we have squandered so much promise? We had made a lifelong commitment to one another. Why were we unable to keep it? We had publicly pronounced that our love would last forever. Why didn't it? What's wrong with us?

The announcement may be greeted with shock and hostility by family and friends. Friends may feel pressured to "choose sides," to make a statement of who is right and who has been wronged. The notion of divorce also compels many of us to examine our own marriages more closely. Seeing the bonds unravel for others heightens our sense of fragility. Divorced men and women may find their married friends avoiding them, moving away from the dreaded possibility of a "life alone."

It is difficult to predict with certainty the effects of divorce on either parent or child. We bring unique personalities, coping styles, and levels of confidence to the potential trauma. Who initiated the divorce? Who took greater control over the situation? Who is more likely to feel as though they are the rejected one? How acrimonious is the separation and divorce process? How much hostility remains after the legalities have been settled? How cooperatively can the former spouses act, particularly with regard to their child's welfare? How much emotional and practical support can one rely upon? What is the age of the child during this transition period? These are but a few of the critical determinants of the disruption one can expect during this crisis.

No two individuals are the same. No two family situations are entirely comparable. Nevertheless, certain stressors often accompany divorce. Economic fortunes and standards of living usually decline for both partners. People are uprooted from their familiar home to new environments. New friends must be made, a new life begun. New skills must be learned. Unanticipated responsibilities must be taken on. A new self-image must be created. Children must cope with their anger, their feelings of abandonment, their feelings of guilt about possibly having caused the dissolution of the marriage, their conflict over loyalty to one or the other parent, their sadness, their grief, their sense of their world having been turned topsy-turvy.

According to the 1993 *World Almanac*, the divorce rate in the United States steadily increased from the turn of the century, with a slight dip in the 1920s, peaking in 1945. Then it dropped steadily until 1960, when it started climbing again, passing the 1945 rate in 1975. The rate peaked in 1980 and has dropped a fair amount.

- Almost half (49%) of all marriages end in divorce.

- For those with a college degree, the proportion is closer to forty percent; for those without a college degree, the proportion is closer to sixty percent.

- Five percent of marriages end within the first year.

- One-third of divorced couples were married between one and four years.

- Early divorcing couples tend to be younger, poorer, and less educated.

- Eighty percent of divorced men remarry.

- Seventy-five percent of divorced women remarry.

How do we explain the stabilization or even slight decline in the incidence of marriages which dissolve? (1) The bulk of the baby-boom generation is past the late twenties, the most likely divorce years. (2) The lower divorce rate may reflect the drop in marriages during the mid-1970s. (3) As adults postpone marriage, their decisions may be more mature, realistic ones. (4) There is a growing, realistic fear of the economic consequences of divorce and the decreasing remarriage rate. (5) For some women, having children is no longer a compelling argument for marriage in the first place. More single women are choosing to raise children alone.

However, other factors contribute to maintaining the high

number of divorces. More women than ever are working outside the home, many of them in more professional careers and surroundings. As their income levels rise, they become more self-reliant and unwilling to tolerate unsatisfying marriages. These working women also have more access to desirable men and, therefore, view themselves as having alternatives. A continuing low birth rate also frees more couples from considerations of the welfare of their children. Our cultural acceptance and normalization of divorce loosen our inhibitions as well.

We have seen the most dramatic rise in the divorce rate among young adults. Two-thirds of all women who divorce do so before the age of thirty. Two immediate consequences of these youthful divorces is that (1) the children involved are younger and (2) the couples are likely to be less financially secure, increasing the stress in their post-divorce life. It is estimated that approximately forty-five percent of all children (one of every three white children, two of every three black children) born in the 1980s will experience their parents' divorce, thirty-five percent will experience a remarriage of at least one parent, and twenty percent will experience a second divorce.

Reasons for Divorce

Emotional divorce occurs long before an actual, physical separation. Spouses withdraw their emotional investment from the marriage and from the other. They focus on each other's weaknesses and deficiencies. Each blames the other for the failure of the marriage and for bringing them such unhappiness. A myriad of feelings are experienced: disillusionment, alienation, anxiety, disbelief, despair, dread, ambivalence, emptiness, anger, inadequacy, and regret, to name a few. After separation and divorce proceedings are initiated, other emotions emerge: depression, rage, self-pity, hopelessness, helplessness, loneliness, relief, and vindictiveness.

Unless a spouse is one of the many who are in denial about the disintegration of the marriage, he/she will not be taken completely by surprise at hearing, "We need to talk. This is not working and I don't think it ever can." It is usually one partner who initiates what they perceive to be the inevitable and unavoidable conclusion. It is usually one partner who articulates that, for them, the damage is irreparable.

But whether one is the initiator or on the receiving end of the pronouncement of intent, the psychological blow of this conclusion is profound. Both partners feel the loss of having invested so much effort and resources in this venture. Both partners decry some of the "best years of my life" which were squandered. Both partners, on some level, feel as though they have failed as adults. ("Maybe I'm not the kind of person who can sustain intimacy," they think. "Maybe I'm not the kind of person who can handle commitment and responsibilities.") Both partners must mourn the death of their marriage and their family unit. Both must grieve over the death of their fantasy. Both must adjust to a new routine, a new life-style. Both must rebuild a workable framework. Both must recover their self-esteem and find an even keel once again.

People do not initiate divorce impulsively, particularly when there are children to be considered. Most of these divorce-bound relationships erode gradually. Even in the case where a spouse discovers an infidelity of the other, the incident is usually the last straw which unmasks previous dissatisfactions. It is also true that affairs are usually symptoms, warning signals of ongoing frustrations. (Most affairs are not entered into impulsively either.) The pros and cons are usually weighed in an agonizing fashion.

The following list includes some of the most common grievances which may cause one or both partners to initiate a divorce:

- Having unrealistic romantic expectations of a marriage.

- An initial idealization of the other which disintegrates over time.

- People change, and younger people are likely to change most. Their interests, values, and expectations diverge.

- One or both partners are too frightened of emotional intimacy and closeness.

- One or both partners communicate ineffectively.

- Sexual incompatibility.

- Difficulty maintaining a long-term commitment. These individuals often have a high need for variety and new stimulation.

- Participating together in fewer and fewer shared activities and interests. These couples lead "parallel lives" as opposed to connected ones.

- Reduced attention and affection.

- Infidelity.

- A lack of sensitivity or an indifference to one's partner's feelings and wishes. This spirals downward as a spouse becomes increasingly unhappy and disconnected from the other.

- Conflicts over power, control, and decision-making.

- An inability to negotiate and problem-solve effectively.

- Conflicts over money.

- Conflicts over issues of independence (i.e., "twoness versus oneness").

- Conflict over in-laws.

- Conflict over child-rearing approaches and practices.

- Physical abuse.

- An inability to respond and adapt to changing circumstances (e.g., the birth of a child).

- External stresses (e.g., financial loss, death of a child) which the couple cannot weather.

Most of the time, more than one of the above factors come into play when deciding to separate. Confounding the picture is the fact that there are comforts one derives from the marriage as well as frustrations. Marriages are usually neither all bad nor all good. But while the process of emotional divorce may have begun because of painful dissatisfaction and disillusionment, it also implicitly insures some new losses as well.

New Post-Separation Equilibriums

For the sake of the children, separated spouses must cooperate in their parenting. But despite this obvious truth, powerful emotions render ex-partners more or less capable of fulfilling this responsibility. In their book *Divorced Families: A Multidisciplinary Developmental View*, Constance Ahrons and Roy Rodgers identify five types of relationships which emerge between former spouses after their break-up.

Perfect Pals. These individuals remain friends. They decide together to live separate lives but, nevertheless, retain a mutual respect for one another. In earlier generations, they probably would not have divorced. While they may have experienced some anger during the separation process, each now considers the other to be a responsible and caring parent. While conflict between them flares intermittently, they are usually able to accommodate to the other's wishes.

Cooperative Colleagues. Ex-husband and wife are no longer friends but retain the ability to cooperate successfully as parents. They may no longer like each other, but they recognize the need to compromise in order to effectively parent and prevent psychological harm to their children. While they experience disagreements, they are, nonetheless, able to prevent those disagreements from escalating into power struggles.

Angry Associates. This former couple is still bitter and resentful about the marriage and the divorce process. They continuously fight about finances, visitation schedules, and custody arrangements. While each remains an active parent, they often force their children into loyalty conflicts.

Fiery Foes. These men and women are unable to coparent. Long after the divorce, their anger has not dissipated. They perceive the other to be "the enemy." While they prolong their legal combat, the children are usually in the middle of their battle and are exhorted to take sides. Under these conditions, the noncustodial parent probably will see his children with decreasing frequency over the years.

Dissolved Duos. There is a cessation of contact between former partners after the divorce. One partner may leave the geographic area. This is, for all intents and purposes, a single-parent family.

Ahrons and Rodgers offer the following illustration of the reactions of each of the relationship types to a child's high school graduation: (1) Perfect Pals plan dinner together, sit together during the ceremony, and perhaps give a joint gift; (2) Cooperative Colleagues both attend the ceremony and, if they sit together, do so under some strain; (3) Angry Associates celebrate separately with the child, sit apart at the ceremony, and avoid contact as much as possible; (4) Fiery Foes exclude one parent from the celebration and perhaps from the ceremony itself, leading the excluded parent to feel hurt and angry; (5) Dissolved Duos do not bother informing the noncustodial parent of the graduation, nor would he or she acknowledge the event if aware of it.

Unfortunately, my experience tells me that there are far too many couples who fall within the description of the last two categories. Their anger and hurt are irrepressible. They are blind to the consequences of their behavior both for their children and for their own long-term mental health. They usually fight a war on two fronts: the emotional and the legal.

Custody Arrangements

In an era of no-fault divorce laws, critical issues still remain to be legally resolved: distribution of property, alimony, child support, and most importantly, child custody. While the law may no longer allow spiteful spouses to stand in the way of a legal dissolution of the marriage, their rage is often played out during the resolution of these other issues.

Since the time of early English common law until the end of the nineteenth century, fathers were generally granted custody of the children when a marriage was dissolved unless it could be established that he was an unfit parent. A wife and offspring were simply considered part of a man's property. Furthermore, fathers were deemed to be economically more capable of providing for their children. The beginning of the women's movement in the late nineteenth century and the Child Labor Laws passed in the early part of this century led to a change in attitudes toward child custody. Once children could no longer be exploited as cheap labor, fathers became more receptive to giving up their children to their ex-wives. In the latter half of the nineteenth century, the criterion of "tender years" was introduced into custody decisions. Mothers were now considered to be in a better position to provide for their children's welfare, particularly in the cases of minor children of "tender years."

In the 1920s, laws were gradually changed so that custody was no longer automatically given to fathers. In many states, the sex of the parent was no longer the determining yardstick for custody decisions. Instead, parental capacity was considered the pre-eminent criterion. In the United States, the dramatic increase in divorce rates as well as the corresponding liberalizing of social attitudes regarding alternative family life-styles led to alterations in custody laws, which came to use "the best interests of the child" in decision making. But because of the "tender years" presumption, a father had to prove a mother grossly unfit before he would be considered the preferred custodian.

By the 1970s, more men began to seek custody of their children. Many courts and state legislatures agreed that the *assumption* of a mother-child arrangement being preferable for the child was sexist and no longer warranted. Parenting situations were now to be judged on a case-by-case basis, with "the interests and welfare of the child" being paramount and without preconceived notions of natural parenting abilities. It has also become more socially acceptable for women to openly acknowledge their lack of maternal interest and defer to the fathers in custody decisions. But despite these trends, the vast majority of children remain with their mothers after separations and divorces.

Until the late 1970s, *sole custody*, in most cases by the mother, remained the most common type of custodial arrangement. One parent is awarded total legal and physical responsibility for the child. The other has visitation rights, plus any additional rights or privileges agreed upon in the divorce settlement. The parent with whom the children live makes most of the important decisions regarding day-to-day matters affecting their welfare. Both parents, however, may participate in such major decisions as education and religious training.

In *divided custody* (or *alternating custody*), the children live about half the time with one parent and half the time with the other. Both parents participate in the important decisions of the child's life. When the child stays with one parent, the other one has visitation privileges. Obviously, this arrangement is only feasible when both parents live in the same school district.

In *split custody*, the children are divided between the two parents. Some live permanently with one parent and some with the other. However, most experts believe it is usually best to keep the children together so they can provide support for one another and a sense of continuity for the family.

Joint custody is an increasingly popular arrangement in which both parents have equal authority with regard to their children's general welfare. In practice, it may take a number of forms. Generally speaking, the most common plan of joint custody is for the children to reside in one home and for the other parent to have access to them. Joint legal custody does not necessarily mean shared parenting on a daily basis. But there is usually no restricted, structured visitation schedule and this distinguishes the arrangement from traditional custodial ones.

Psychologically, joint custody is probably the healthiest and most desirable of the various custodial plans. In some states, such as California, joint legal custody is presumed in all divorces unless a ruling is made to the contrary. Joint custody helps avoid a situation where the noncustodial parent feels extraneous. It also avoids the sole custody situation where one parent is placed in a position of authority over the other. Because of a greater freedom of access to the children, the joint custodial arrangement may also reduce the hostility of the noncustodial parent toward the ex and, therefore, also provide more motivation to continue financial support of all of them.

In a variation of joint custody called *joint physical custody*, both parents take part in day-to-day care of and decision making for their children, although the parents live separately. The children may move between households every week or every month or perhaps spend weekdays with one parent and weekends with the other. (Note that physical custody relates to the parent with whom the child primarily lives. Legal custody refers to decision-making powers.)

Courts are increasingly urging shared custody arrangements in hopes that bitter, drawn-out custody battles can be avoided. Judges want children to have the benefit of contact with both parents and realize that a shared-custody parent is more apt to remain involved (both financially and psychologically) and less likely to drift away. They also hope to reduce the stress on the single parent who is suddenly confronted with the burden of assuming parenthood alone.

However, the eminent child psychiatrist Richard Gardner emphasizes that joint custody is only viable if: (1) both parents are equally capable of assuming the responsibilities of child rearing, (2) the parents have demonstrated their capacity to cooperate reasonably in matters pertaining to raising their children, and (3) the child's school situation is not disrupted by moving from home to home.

Because the animosity between parents may peak at the time of their divorce, a joint custodial arrangement might better wait until a point in the future when tempers have cooled and cooperative efforts are more realistic. Sometimes, a court will make a joint custodial arrangement temporary and finalize it only after the parents have demonstrated that they can make it work.

The determination of custody is tricky. Some men (and fewer women), for example, seek custody even though they know that their ex-spouse can provide more effective and emotionally supportive parenting. They may use this issue as leverage in negotiating other outstanding matters (e.g., property division). In their anger, custody rights become a convenient weapon with which to hold their former partner hostage and inflict punishment. Some men indicate an interest in custody as a means of alleviating their guilt for having initiated the separation that tore their family asunder.

When the degree of anger interferes with the ability of the parents to mutually arrive at rational choices in the best interests of the child, custodial decisions are left to the courts, usually during an acrimonious, adversarial litigation process. Children are often exposed to the sordid details of their parents' marriage and placed in untenable positions of having to state their preferred custodian. A final determination is made by an overloaded judge who is not familiar with either of the parents or their children. Because of the ineffectiveness and potential harm of this approach, professional mediators (often a team made up of a mental health specialist and a lawyer) sometimes assist spouses in arriving at these decisions outside of the litigious process.

Custody battles frequently become intertwined with financial ones. Both areas of contention may become tinged by desires for revenge and future control. Traditionally, the man has been ordered by the courts to sustain his ex-wife and children at their predivorce economic level. Alimony may continue for life if the ex-wife does not remarry. More recently, there has been a trend toward an equitable division of property instead of automatic alimony.

When Dad Moves Out

Mothers are awarded custody of minor children in approximately ninety percent of divorces. A child's contact with the noncustodial father is largely determined by the visitation arrangements in the divorce settlement. A father may ultimately see his children regularly (on a weekly or, more rarely, on a daily basis), intermittently, or not at all. A common pattern allows for noncustodial fathers and their children to get together on weekends, some holidays, some school vacations, and perhaps, one evening during the week.

Just as angry fathers may often withhold financial support as a means of lashing out, enraged mothers may use their position of physical custodian to deprive their ex-partner of contact with his family. She may "forget" about a previously arranged outing of father and children. Or a father may find that his children are never dressed or ready to go when he arrives at the appointed hour. (This can, of course, work both ways. An angry father, for example, may "forget" to pick his kids up, thus forcing the mother to cancel her eagerly awaited plans on her free day.)

Despite how ambivalent he may have been or how painful the decision became, a husband who initiates separation has made an active choice. Feeling powerless, rejected, and furious that he has broken the commitment they made to one another, his ex-wife may expect the children to share her rage. Richard Gardner has coined the term "parental alienation syndrome" to describe the absolute hatred and continuous vilification of one parent (usually the father) and idolization of the other (usually the mother) by a child caught up in this dynamic. There is a complete disregard for the feelings or point of view of the hated parent and a concomitant total absence of gratitude for anything that parent may have provided in the past or continues to provide in the present. Oftentimes, the implacable detestation is directed toward the father's entire extended family as well. Presents are refused, cards remain unopened, and telephone overtures are hung up on.

If you are a noncustodial father, you have more than self-blame to cope with. For you, divorce arouses insecurities, fears of loneliness, and feelings of isolation. As you lose continuous contact with your family, you are also deprived of the meaning and structure of your life. You no longer feel needed in the everyday world of your children. When you pick your children up, you must deal with mourning your previous role and relationship and grieve the loss of your dreams and plans for your former family, which may have included having grandchildren. You must periodically cope with events which your intact family should have attended (e.g., graduations, weddings, birthday parties). You must now support two households instead of one. Geographic relocation may cut the physical tie between you and your children.

Many other factors may influence your desire to remain connected to your children on an ongoing basis. How close a relationship did you have with your children before the separation? How do you feel about having contact with your ex? How comfortable are you with being a "visiting dad"? How comfortable are your children seeing you under these circumstances? What are the ages of the children at separation (e.g., adolescents may have less time for you, while infants may feel to you like too much work)? How do your children make you feel when they are with you? Are they happy to see you? Angry at you because of what "you did to their mom"? How comfortable or adept are you and your children at talking about feelings which have arisen as a result of the breakup? How freely and easily does your ex allow you access to your children?

You may become *more* involved with your children after a divorce. Perhaps an unsatisfying marriage had kept you away from family involvement. You may feel as though you need your children more than ever in order to provide meaning to your life and fill the void created by the breakup. You may feel a keener sense of responsibility to provide as much psychological support for your children as possible because of the mess you have placed them in. As you spend entire, uninterrupted weekends with your children, the quality of the time spent together may lead to an enhanced closeness. Fathers may actually interact more with their children after divorces than before. With idealized images now removed and all concerned feeling more vulnerable, fathers and children may learn more and understand more about each other than ever before. You may value your time with your children more than you had previously. You and your children may cling to one another for a sense of safety and security.

Having frequent contact with your children can provide both you and your kids with reassurance and structure. Having a visitation schedule allows for pleasant anticipation. (Not following through on prearranged visits likewise fosters disappointment and mistrust.) After moving out, you should maintain at least daily telephone contact with your children and emphasize to them your accessibility should they wish to call you. By way of retaining a strong connection between you, you should tell your children about the ongoing events in your life so that they do not feel that you have begun a "brand new life," one which implicitly excludes them. Your kids should be encouraged to sleep over at your house so that you do not simply seem like a visitor when you arrive to take them on outings. (If possible, the children should have their own room at your house so they will feel it is their home as well.)

As a noncustodial father, you may have difficulty maintaining your role as disciplinarian. Setting unpopular limits may risk losing a child's love and approval. Guilt over the divorce may lead to overindulgent behavior. And guilt may cause you to rationalize that indulgence: "They're going through a difficult time. I want them to feel good. I want them to feel loved." A father may attempt to buy his child's loyalty, particularly if he is locked in a struggle for affection with his ex. He may want to insure that his children view him as "the good guy."

For some fathers, particularly those who were previously extremely close with their children, the intermittent visitation schedule brought on by the divorce may prove too painful and frustrating. They may, then, withdraw from familial involvement. In general, often because of their ex's vindictiveness or the pain of repeated separations from the children, noncustodial fathers have less and less contact with their children as time passes. Because of their lack of parenting skills, visits with children may prove anxiety-provoking and unsatisfying for both fathers and offspring. Fathers may look forward to beginning a new life, free of the unpleasant reminders of their false start. As their children demonstrate obvious adjustment to the divorce, they may also tell themselves that their frequent presence might simply be disruptive rather than helpful.

Noncustodial fathers who have not remarried have the most regular contact with their children. But the vast majority of divorced individuals do marry again. Often, this remarriage leads to diminished closeness with one's children, particularly in cases where the father has children with his new spouse. Of course, a father could be immeasurably helped by a new wife who is extremely supportive of his relationship with his children from a previous marriage. But unfortunately, many new spouses in this situation feel jealous and threatened by the possibility of "dual loyalties." They may subtly or explicitly offer some form of the ultimatum, "them or me."

Fathers who fall behind in their child support payments often begin to avoid their children. They may feel guilty and unworthy to be active fathers. Or they may lack the desire to parent, and their lack of financial responsibility reflects this deficiency. These fathers show up occasionally with stories of why their presence had been impossible sooner. Testimony to a child's need to love and to feel loved, sons and daughters are often thrilled at the appearance, as they tenaciously cling to their fantasy of an idealized parent.

The Custodial Parent

Many men who have taken an active role in bringing up their children simply are not willing to give them up when a marriage or relationship dissolves. And with fewer moms staying home full-time, judges are determining that the best interests of the child may not necessarily be as clear-cut as they once were. Men raising their children on their own have climbed from ten percent of single parents in 1980 to almost fifteen percent in 1991. Furthermore, these dads are not the stereotypical wealthy widowers or fathers raising only boys or older children. Approximately two-thirds of single fathers are divorced. Almost one-third of single dads are caring for preschoolers, and forty-four percent of the children for whom single dads have custody are girls.

As women increasingly enter careers and courts follow the cultural trend against gender bias, men will be granted more sole and joint custody. Today, however, special circumstances must often be proven. Single fathers are usually held to a higher standard of potential parenting ability than mothers. In order to gain custody of their children, they must often demonstrate that the mothers are emotionally debilitated or addicted to drugs or, in some incontrovertible manner, unable to fulfill the minimal duties of motherhood. Fathers may be preferred by the courts if they have remarried and the ex-spouse has not and if their economic circumstances are clearly more stable.

If you retain custody of your children, you may be spared the simultaneous loss of your couple status and your family. Children provide ongoing, visible reminders of your raison d'etre. They provide structure, responsibility, involvement, and pleasure. Fathers in this position are less likely to suffer a sense of alienation or isolation and may feel less incentive to frantically enter the dating world while they are still trying to regain their emotional equilibrium.

Nevertheless, the custodial father is in for a stressful time. Because he must now run a household *and* support his ex-wife, his economic pressures have increased. He must cope with his own emotional distress and help his children adjust to their changed circumstances. He will probably be embroiled in an ongoing conflict with his ex-spouse, at least for a period of time. His career trajectory may stall as the demands on his time require a reordering of priorities. While his colleagues may provide lip-service support, he may also be ridiculed for "taking on woman's work" or "becoming a mommy."

When the custodial parent is feeling particularly lonely, rejected, unfairly treated, and helpless, she or he may turn to the children for solace. A daughter may suddenly be thrust into the role of confidante, pal, or even parent. The child, in these circumstances, is not only suddenly expected to become more self-sufficient, but must also cope with the needs of her mother or father. There is often an implicit request that the child grow up quickly so that she can understand what the aggrieved parent is experiencing. Older children may be expected to assume greater responsibilities for household duties and for their younger siblings.

The custodial parent who is particularly unmotivated, ineffective, or unsuccessful at resocialization may foster a dependent and almost romantic attachment to a child. Comments such as, "You'll have to be the man of the house," may arouse dormant oedipal feelings in a child, which can provoke considerable anxiety. As the boundary between parent and child roles becomes blurred, a son or daughter is denied the security of a protector, someone who is in charge, someone who can set limits which are in the best interests of the child.

Overwhelmed by losses, bitter at the turn her life has taken, the custodial parent may vent some of her rage toward a child who is seen as the embodiment of the absent parent. Filled with self-pity, this mother may now exclusively view her child as a burden and demand a self-sufficiency which the child is not up to. Unable to move forward with her life and remaining mired in her wrath and feelings of victimization, this mother forces her child to essentially be on her own.

Children of Divorce

Children survive divorce. But it is a painful process for them. And neither parents nor children can emerge from divorce entirely unscathed.

Initially, children cannot fully comprehend what is occurring. "Separation?" "Mommy doesn't love daddy anymore?" "We're not going to be living together?" "What do you mean?" Unless they are older and there has been physical violence or ugly, open conflict between parents, children do not react to the news with relief. On the contrary, the overwhelming feelings they experience are vulnerability, anxiety, and powerlessness. As Judith Wallerstein has written: "To the child, divorce signifies the collapse of the structure that provides support and protection. The child reacts as to the cutting of his or her lifeline."

Sometimes a child's reaction to divorce is delayed. Younger children may not grasp the concept. Older children may deny reality as a means of magically reassuring themselves that their worlds will not be torn apart. And when they can no longer effectively dispute the obvious, they often fantasize about the reunion and reconstitution of the family. For many children, these fantasies persist for years. Boys and girls ride an emotional roller coaster as their hopes are repeatedly disappointed.

Children want their parents to stay together. Unless it is obviously and exceedingly traumatic, they prefer to live with conflict because they have learned to adapt to it in some manner. Divorce means the unknown and raises the specter of permanent loss.

The feelings of abandonment stirred by the separation are often increased by the parents' preoccupations with their own reactions and their lack of emotional availability. A mother or father may displace frustration and anger meant for their ex onto the child, further contributing to feelings of rejection. The anxiety created is often manifested in a refusal to attend school. At this time, a child may refuse to stay with a babysitter or even visit a friend's house for fear of being permanently left alone. The regressive behavior (e.g., thumb sucking, bedwetting, clinging) we observe in some children signifies their attempt to reassure themselves, to move back to a more familiar and secure point in time.

Children of divorce are understandably angry. They are not only angry for what has been taken away from them but also because they had no choice in the matter. This is something which is happening *to* them. Some children are able to express explicitly, "I hate you for messing up my life." Others are too afraid of further repercussions, further abandonment, to share their feelings. Sometimes their anger is primarily directed toward the noncustodial parent ("You caused this!"), although sometimes the custodial parent is the target simply because she is more available.

Oftentimes, a child's anger is turned on himself and causes depression. We tend to search for explanations of events and frequently find them (realistically or not) in our own perceived shortcomings. A child may feel worthless, undeserving of love, and perhaps, even the cause of the breakup.

When a child feels *sadness*, he is unable to derive pleasure from his usual activities. In almost all such cases, these sad children gradually improve and reinvest in life.

Depressed children, however, demonstrate more severe reactions: a loss of appetite, apathy, helplessness, hopelessness, self-criticism, withdrawal, and low frustration tolerance. The potential for depression in children of divorce may be influenced by how close and/or dependent a relationship had existed with the noncustodial parent before the separation, as well as how depressed over the divorce the custodial parent remains. A recent longitudinal study in northern California followed 131 children who ranged in ages from three to eighteen at the time of their parents' separation. At the five-year mark, one-third of these youngsters suffered from moderate to severe depression. A national survey revealed that compared to children living in a two-parent family, children of divorce also evidenced more difficulties with learning: They attended school more erratically and they had a higher drop-out rate.

Guilt is another result of the anger we direct at ourselves. Children of divorce commonly worry that they were, in some way, instrumental in causing the insurmountable difficulties that led to the divorce. For example, if parents had openly and severely disagreed about child-rearing approaches, a son or daughter may latch on to this evidence as proof of his or her responsibility for the parents' irreconcilable differences. Perhaps a child learned that he was never wanted by one parent and that this disagreement caused considerable tension. Perhaps parents made continual reference to feeling overwhelmed by "responsibilities."

At times, out of guilt, at times, out of love, children worry about their distressed parents. ("Who will cook for my dad? Who will take care of him?" "Who will take care of my mom? Will she be able to make it on her own? Will she be able to handle all of this by herself?") These concerns further fuel their fantasies and actual attempts to mend the broken marriage.

Divorce and Children at Different Ages

Parents who are considering divorce often ask, "When would be the best time for my child?" Unfortunately, there probably is no "best time" for most children to experience this breaking apart. Children always feel somewhat vulnerable. Children always need emotional security. Children always need models with whom they can identify. But in general, younger children are more destabilized because, while they sense the omnipresent despair, they are unable to completely understand what is transpiring (which may, for example, lead them to blame themselves for the separation of mommy and daddy) and because of their greater dependence on their parents.

In response to the separation, children may manifest emotional symptoms immediately or sometime down the road. However, we have noted particular problems which seem to characterize the various developmental stages.

Preschool Children. For the preschooler, seeing his parents leave one another implies the possibility of his own abandonment. Routine separations from the custodial parent (e.g., at bedtime) may arouse inordinate anxiety. He may regress in his behavior (e.g., lose bowel or bladder control, act excessively clingy) or become demanding and aggressive with his parents, siblings, and peers. He yearns for the lost parent and may fantasize a great deal about him or speak to his invisible presence for reassurance.

Five to Eight Years Old. The somewhat older child may present obvious signs of depression. He may become withdrawn and uncommunicative. He may refuse to go to school. He longs for the reuniting of his parents and is also concerned about the welfare of the one who has moved out. He may develop problems as a means of bringing them together again. Children in this age group often imagine having precipitated the divorce and are likely to feel unwarranted guilt. They may develop an irrational fear of being replaced in their parents' lives by another child.

Nine to Twelve Years Old. Preadolescents are likely to express anger toward one or both parents for what they are being put through. They are also furious because their image of an all-good, all-knowing, all-protective parent has been shattered. They grieve the loss of their intact family. They may see one parent as the victim and the other as the bad guy. Particularly when caught up in custody battles, they are likely to feel conflicts of loyalty. They may become so angry with one parent (usually the noncustodial one) that they reject all contact and identification with him (e.g., if a son previously enjoyed playing chess with his father, he may give up the game entirely). School performance and peer relationships may deteriorate. Older children may display empathy and care for a distressed parent.

Adolescents. These children may become depressed. They may act out their anger by defying social conventions. (In children of this age, it is important to distinguish the reactions to the divorce from the usual acts of adolescent rebellion.) Preoccupied with issues of morality, a child may judge one parent harshly and idealize the other. Because of their enhanced feelings of insecurity, a child may become more compliant for fear of further abandonment. Many adolescents also respond to this crisis by growing in maturity and independence.

Eighteen to Twenty-two Years Old. These children worry about their parents (especially their mothers). They become anxious about their own future, particularly with regard to marriage. In the heat of the crisis, they may vow not to marry nor to have children of their own.

Other Influences

Gender matters too. When a divorce occurs during a child's preschool or preadolescent years, boys seem to fare worse than girls. Perhaps because they are likely to remain living with their custodial mothers, girls seem to bounce back more easily than boys, who lose their same-sex identification figure. When divorce occurs during adolescence, girls may be more likely to get into social trouble as they experiment with relationships in which they seek the attention of men. Girls may also more acutely grapple with fears of commitment and betrayal by members of the opposite sex.

Finally, a child's birth order position in the family may be related to additional stress. A firstborn may feel more responsible for the welfare of not only his parents, but his siblings as well. A last-born might have more difficulty leaving home at the right age because she views her departure as another abandonment of the custodial parent.

Unfortunately, most children going through a divorce lose the guidance and support of their most important allies—their parents—just when they need them the most. It is common for mothers and fathers to be less capable of parenting both before and right after the actual divorce. Their preoccupation with their loss of self-esteem, a sense of helplessness, anger, and feelings of being overburdened render them less sensitive to the needs of their children and less capable of deriving pleasure from the parent-child relationship. For most, two to four years must pass before they achieve a constructive resolution of the unleashed emotions and adapt to the divorce-related changes in their life-styles. Some people, of course, become stuck in their self-blame or bitterness. They are unable to romantically connect with different partners or to proceed with new, independent lives. They remain caught up in old grievances and continue to engage in tit-for-tat retributions with their exes. Unfortunately, their feelings about their former spouses continue to interfere with their parenting behavior, which should always be ruled by the best interests of the children.

Parents worry about whether their divorce will irreparably damage their children. Indeed, when we see sons and daughters of divorce grapple with emotional difficulties, it is often impossible to tell whether those difficulties started with predivorce familial tension or the trauma of the separation or the conflict which occurred after the divorce. Divorce is not a single event which occurs at a precise moment in time. An entire childhood and adolescence may be dominated by family tension and upheaval.

The most stressed children are those caught up in acrimonious legal battles as parents maneuver for custody, visitation rights, child support, and alimony. If anger and vindictiveness predominate the post-divorce relationship, if a child is poorly informed about the pending separation, if a child is not emotionally supported and understood during the process, if a child is coopted as a parental ally, if a child's relationship with one parent is disrupted or interfered with, or if a child feels rejected or responsible for the divorce, he is likely to experience psychological harm.

When parents anticipate and plan for the psychological, social, and economic consequences before separation, when parents provide reassurance and understanding to their children, when both parents maintain ongoing, healthy relationships with their children, when the noncustodial parent is encouraged by his ex-spouse to remain involved with his children, sons and daughters of divorce will be less likely to experience enduring, debilitating distress. The quality of the parents' relationship after the divorce can greatly diminish the effects of the separation itself.

Children bounce back best from divorce when their parents are able to resolve their anger and set aside their conflict, when the visiting parent remains connected so that they do not feel rejected, and when they have an extended supportive network (e.g., peers, siblings, extended family) available for them. Of course, whatever personality assets and mature coping mechanisms the child already possesses will help immeasurably as well. But do not expect any child's feelings about the divorce to go away in days, weeks, or months.

Today's children see divorce all around them. In some ways, the notion and the reality of divorce have become normalized. But the ubiquitousness of the phenomenon has also subtly increased every child's sense of vulnerability. Children ask themselves: What causes divorce? Could divorce happen to me if I behaved badly? Perhaps you have been asked out of the clear blue by your child, "Are you and mommy ever getting a divorce?"

How to Tell Your Children

Parents dread the moment when they must inform children about the separation. They want to do it right. They want to do it in a way that will be least harmful to their children. They want to be able to cope with their own discomfort. And they want to get it over with.

The following are some guidelines for when, how, and what

to tell your children. I have also included some commonly accepted wisdom about anticipating and responding to your child's reactions.

- *Do not mention separation to your children until the decision is a definite one.* Begin the discussion about one or two weeks before the actual, physical move. This period will allow children the opportunity to ask questions and clarify future arrangements. It should also be used to encourage children to speak of their feelings about the upcoming breakup. Do not have The Talk much before the two-week guideline, as it allows time for children to raise their hopes that the decision can be changed, that their parents will stay together, that their world will not be shattered.

- *Children should be told by both parents together.* You want to clearly communicate that this is a *mutual* decision (and that, despite the divorce, the future will involve mutual parenting as well). You want to implicitly and explicitly communicate that no one parent was responsible either for the difficulties which led to the separation or the actual decision to part ways. Remember that your children need to continue to see both of you in a positive light.

- *The discussion should include all of the children.* While receiving the news, they can provide support for one another. The older may comfort the younger. It also helps them begin the process of facing the situation together, which will be an important support as time goes on. If children are told separately, they may wonder, "What is the other being told that is being kept from me?"

- *Do not lie to your children.* But you need not tell them the whole truth. Leave out the potentially unnerving, tawdry details.

- *You must dispel any child's belief that he somehow caused the divorce.* Despite not loving each other anymore, parents must reassure their children of their constant love for each child. Emphasize that loving either parent will not jeopardize their place in the heart of the other.

- *Be sure that you do not say anything which might nourish their fantasies of reconciliation.*

- *Urge your child to ask any questions he may have at any time.* If a child repeatedly asks the same questions, he is often simply attempting to master his separation anxiety and the reality of his new world.

- *Reassure them of their continuing contact with the noncustodial parent and his extended family.* Tell your child about the details of visitation arrangements. "I'll still be coming to all your soccer games" instills in the child a sense that his world is not completely crumbling. Actually take your children to see where daddy will be living so they do not fear that he will disappear.

Dr. Fitzhugh Dodson, in his book, *How to Father,* offers an excellent model for opening the discussion with your children.

We have something to tell you and it is unhappy news. When we first married we were happy together, but we're not happy anymore. Probably you've noticed that we haven't been getting along very well together lately. We have decided that it will be best if we don't live together anymore and so we are getting a divorce. That means we won't be husband and wife. But we want you to know that this divorce has nothing to do with you children. You did not cause it. It is entirely due to the fact that your father and mother are unhappy together and we've decided we don't want to be married to one another. Your father will live somewhere else, but you will visit him often. You will stay with your mother, and your father will send her money each month to help take care of you.

Although we will no longer be married, one thing will never change. Your father will always be your father and he will always love you. Your mother will always be your mother and she will always love you. That's one thing you can always count on. Now if you have any questions about the divorce and what it will mean to you, you can ask us now or any time you want to.

Some mental health professionals encourage parents to tell their children about their own feelings (e.g., anger, frustration, sadness, fear) and difficulties concerning their decision. I disagree. At this point in time, children's psychological resources will be maximally strained. Children must not be made to feel more anxious or compelled to take care of their parents. On the contrary, they already feel as though their worlds are falling apart and are entitled to whatever steadying influence you can provide. Children may also pick up your emotional cues and incorporate them in their own reactions. For example, if a parent feels ashamed of what is taking place, a child may also undeservedly mimic that shame.

Children will react to the news in a myriad of ways. They may ask many questions or they may be silent. They may immediately grasp the concept or they may deny its reality. They may attempt to cope with their distress by seeking information and reassurance ("Will I still have my birthday party next week?"), or they may be afraid to inquire about details because they irrationally feel responsible for what has transpired. Because a child in this circumstance is likely to feel rejected by his parents, he must repeatedly be reassured of both parents' continuing love and the fact that he was not at fault in any way. And because children will attempt to discover which parent is to blame, both parents must continue to emphasize their joint responsibility for their unsuccessful marriage and decision to divorce.

Parents must help their children articulate their feelings about the divorce and their grief over the death of their family as they knew it. Children will understandably feel angry. They have a right to two parents. Even if they do not express their anger, they may, nonetheless, feel guilty for having it. Children under the age of five, for example, experience what psychologists term "magical thinking." They believe their angry thoughts can actually harm the objects of their hostility. This reasoning may obviously increase the guilt they may already feel about being a bad boy who has somehow caused all of this to happen. Children going through divorce may have nightmares of intruders harming them. This scenario usually reflects both a projection of their anger and their enhanced sense of vulnerability.

A structured visitation schedule must be planned and implemented. It must be specific (e.g., "Father will take the children out every Friday night," as opposed to, "Father will take the children out one night each week"). If possible, the noncustodial parent should see his children together and separately. Particularly immediately following the separation, the noncustodial parent should encourage continuous, daily contact, even if it is simply a telephone call. The conversations need not always be serious and emotionally intense. You want to communicate to your children that you love them, that you are there for them, and that they are not powerless to maintain contact with you.

Caught in the Middle

Children's post-divorce adjustment is directly related to their parents' post-divorce adjustment. When outrage and a profound sense of betrayal dominate a parent's life, she will be blinded to the best interests of the child. Out of control, she will invariably force her child to become caught up in her ongoing battle for vindication. Smoldering anger can cripple a parent's ability to move on successfully with her life.

This anger may linger for years. It seems to be most pronounced in women who had been married to their exes for extended periods ("I gave him the best years of my life") and who find it difficult to adjust to their new single lives. They may envy exes who establish romantic relationships or marry, who are doing "better" post-divorce than they are. They want their former spouses to be feeling pain, not pleasure. They want their former spouses to miss them, to indicate in some way that their marriage did, indeed, have some meaning. They want their ex-spouses to regret having initiated the divorce.

Resentments get played out in arguments over custody, visitation, and alimony. Divorced parents must ask themselves: When I have an impulse to deny my children to my ex-spouse, what is really going on? During this traumatic time for children, it is more important than ever for parents to present a united front, to indicate to their children that the other is to be respected and loved. Children have a profound sense of loyalty to both parents. They will, therefore, inevitably become anxious and conflicted when one denigrates the other.

Bitter parents may force their children to choose. Who do you love? Who do you hate? Who is right? Who is wrong? They enlist their children as allies in their war against their ex. They send messages via their children ("You tell your father that if he's late one more time, then. . . ."). They enlist their children as spies in order to gather information (usually about money or dating) concerning their ex. They keep tabs on their ex in order to find justification for their anger or to remain psychologically connected to him or her. Whatever the circumstances, parents should *never* use their children as a go-between or ask them to betray their mother or father. On the contrary, children must be helped to say, "I don't want to get involved in your arguments" or "If you have something to say to him, tell him yourself."

Divorce Therapy

Particularly when children are involved, you must do everything you possibly can to make your marriage work. You must enlist all of your empathy, all of your patience, all of your compassion, and all of your negotiating skills in resolving conflict and individual dissatisfaction. You must go the extra one hundred miles. The personal distress and agony a divorce will cause your children will inevitably lead you to question whether or not you did the right thing. If you have done everything possible to save your marriage, you will, at least, firmly believe that you had no other option.

Conjoint divorce therapy helps divorcing couples disengage and, hopefully, refrain from continuing or escalating their conflict. It helps parents make the social, emotional, and psychological adjustments necessary in their transition to divorce and the dissolution of their original family unit. If for no other reason, divorced parents should seek counseling if they are having difficulty cooperating in their child rearing.

Divorce therapy provides other opportunities as well:

- It can facilitate the growth of each individual after the divorce.

- It can help you mourn the loss of the relationship and resolve your anger toward your ex so you can move on to a new relationship, unencumbered by emotional baggage.

- It can bring you to accept the fact that the marriage is indeed over. It can nurture the development of the separate identity you need to get on with your life.

- It can help you make peace with your ex-spouse so that you can have a smooth, functional relationship with regard to the children.

- It can insure that you are not held back by persistent self-blame, guilt, anger, and doubt.

- It can help you understand why you chose your mate in the first place and your own contribution to the dysfunctional marriage.

- It can assist you in finding a new social support system.

- It can make you sensitive to not becoming overly dependent on your children, to not enlisting them as allies against your ex, and to not using them as a substitute for an adult life of your own.

- It can help you walk the fine line between asserting your legal rights and not using custody or visitation issues to punish your ex.

Although it is difficult to do so, parents owe it to themselves and their children to resolve their feelings of anger, vengeance, and rage toward one another. Indications that you are reaching that goal may be your ability to (1) articulate your contribution to the failure of the marriage and (2) to tell the other what you appreciated about the life you shared together.

Beginning Again

After going through a divorce, you may feel like a failure at love. You may be riddled with self-doubt about your ability to be intimate or to sustain a commitment. You may feel insecure and inadequate because of the criticism heaped on you by your ex over the years. The separation from your family has left you without an anchor, adrift, and lonely. Legal wrangling and financial pressures have you on edge. You worry about your children and your own ability to survive. And you wonder, Am I still a desirable man?

Your friends tell you, "It's important to move on. Start circulating." You may have heard that it's a single man's dream out there, that the ratio of desirable single women to desirable single men is very much in your favor. And so you contemplate the strange concept of "dating" again.

A word of advice. Wait. Wait until you have regained your

balance. Wait until you are less angry, less disappointed. Wait until you are emotionally disconnected from your ex. Wait so that you can devote your energy and attention to easing the transition for your children. Wait so that you have the time to more calmly consider the kind of woman, the kind of relationship, and the kind of life you would like to have the next time around.

When you do begin to date, be prepared for the anger of others. Your children will be angry because you are dashing their hopes for their parents' reconciliation, and because they fear being replaced in your heart by another. They may feel that you are being disloyal to them and (still) to their mother. They may dread a final and absolute abandonment.

Your ex-spouse's anger will probably flare as well when you start dating, particularly if she is finding it difficult to begin a new social life. She will inevitably respond to your new girlfriend with, You got divorced for this?! The notion of "you are mine," of marital possession, dies hard.

Finding the right person for you is difficult enough. Finding the right one for you and your children becomes an even more daunting task. How will she relate to my children? you wonder. How will she relate to my children after she is no longer intent on making a good impression on me and on them? How will she treat them when she is my wife? Most women are not thrilled about becoming entangled with a man who brings children with him. ("This man not only comes with emotional baggage," they may think, "but physical baggage as well.")

You need not hide the fact that you are dating from your children. But you should not put them through the emotional ordeal of meeting your casual acquaintances. Introduce a new partner to your children only when the relationship is clearly a serious one. When they meet this rival for your affection, it would be a good idea to reassure them of the incomparably special place which they occupy in your life.

Parents agonize over "what would be best" for their children. Fortunately, the prospect of social stigma no longer keeps spouses together who can only give their children a tension-filled, anxiety-laden home environment. Furthermore, "staying together for the sake of the children" was often just a rationalization which masked personal insecurities such as the fear of being alone or the prospect of financial hardship. Clearly, it is far better for a child to grow up in a loving, single-parent household (with, hopefully, the noncustodial parent involved on a continuous basis) than one which is either rancorous or devoid of affection between husband and wife.

If you are recently separated, you must resolve your feelings of guilt or failure so that you can be a more emotionally available parent to your children. Because of their enhanced sense of vulnerability following the separation of their mother and father, children need their parents more than ever. Despite the dissolution of their family unit, they struggle to retain a psychological sense of family. It is important for both ex-spouses to iron out their conflicts so they can be supportive of each other's role as parent. Your commitment to each other may have ended, but your responsibility to your children goes on.

CHAPTER ELEVEN

Stepdads

Men and women who divorce may be bitter, disillusioned, and disheartened. But they don't give up. Approximately eighty-four percent of divorced men and seventy-seven percent of divorced women eventually remarry, most of them within five years of the dissolution of their previous marriages. Forty percent of all marriages are remarriages for at least one partner.

The remarriage rate is highest for those in the youngest age brackets and declines sharply in the older age groups. Young women with less education hasten to remarry and consistently represent the highest proportion of any group to do so. College-educated, childless women are the least likely to remarry. For the economically independent, unencumbered woman, remarriage appears less attractive than it does for those who see themselves as having few options. But even within this privileged cohort, sixty percent eventually retie the knot. In general, however, the longer a divorced individual remains single, the less likely that person will be to try again.

Why are men more likely to remarry than women? Two

significant factors come into play: (1) Men tend to marry younger women and, therefore, have a larger pool of available mates to draw from; (2) Because women usually have physical custody of their children, there is a complex, frightening barrier perceived by prospective partners.

When men remarry, they often acquire a package deal. One-third of all children growing up today will live in a stepfamily household before they reach their eighteenth birthday. And there are over twenty million stepparents in the United States. The stepfamily configuration is complicated and fragile, beset by both internal and external tensions. While sixty percent of all remarriages fail, the figure jumps to seventy-five percent when children are involved.

One would hope that adults enter second marriages with more realistic expectations, a greater appreciation of what it takes to make a commitment work, and more forceful attractions to mates who possess the qualities conducive to life-long partnerships. Yet, remarried people divorce at a higher rate than those in first marriages. Presumably, many simply repeat their past mistakes in their choices of spouses. But when you inherit a stepfamily, you take on increased financial pressures, intense jealousies from many quarters, new resentments, and even greater demands on one's time and patience.

A successful second marriage has the potential to rebuild self-esteem. You have the opportunity to discover that you are, indeed, capable of loving and worthy of being loved. Your stepchildren have the opportunity to view and be influenced by a loving, interminable relationship. If your second try fails, however, self-recrimination and self-doubt will become even more deeply embedded. And when stepchildren observe another failed marriage, and experience another dissolved parent-child bond, their mistrust of commitment will be reinforced.

On one level, prospective stepchildren make an assessment of their potential gains and losses attendant to the acquisition of a "new father" (and, perhaps, "new brothers and sisters"). Some children are delighted at the prospect, as it may mean more financial resources, fewer obligations to serve as a companion/ helper to their biological parent, and greater freedom to live independent lives. But most boys and girls will primarily feel apprehension about the ramifications of having this interloper invade their lives, resentment at having their biological father displaced, and fear of losing their mother (on the heels of just having lost their father) to a stranger.

Realistic Expectations

Children bring a painful, angry, and disappointed history of divorce or death along when they merge into a stepfamily. As a result, you cannot rush the stepparent-stepchild relationship. Indeed, you may be discouraged at how slowly your new family warms to you. Older children are particularly resistant to accepting a stepfather. Most adolescents are in a rebellious mode to start with. And the older the child, the more likely he is to feel, "I did okay without you so far. I don't need you now." Your stepchildren will be leery of your intentions and reliability. They will test you by being rude and uncommunicative. They will want to gauge your staying power.

While you are not their natural father, you can be an involved father. Your stepchildren will be able to tell if you are just going through the motions of being a parent. They can sense your resentment of "this extra burden." They will know if you wish they would disappear (as they initially wish you would disappear). If you want to have a close relationship with your stepchildren, you must make the same commitment of patience, caring, and time as you would with your biological children.

Let your stepchildren develop a relationship with you at their own pace. Let them know you would welcome one. You can create goodwill by spending time alone with them, indicating that you value them apart from their mother. You can demonstrate you care by mentoring them. Loving feelings in your step-children will hopefully arise from living with you day after day and seeing your continuing concern for them. You can't rush love. You can't demand love.

Expect ambivalence in both your stepchildren and in yourself. Instant parenthood does not imply instant love. We simply don't feel the same way about someone else's children as we do about our own. So don't be dishonest. Don't prematurely say, "I love you." In fact, you may never love them. What is most important is that you treat them considerately.

Your stepchildren may not love you either. They may never think of you as their father. (Particularly if their father is still alive, have them call you by your first name. They already have a "dad.") What you should expect is that they treat you with respect and consideration as well. There is cause for optimism, however. What frequently occurs is that as the connection between you and their mom solidifies, your stepchildren will mirror their mother's feelings for you, and consequently, they will begin relating to you more as their parent. When they see you loving the person they are most tied to, they will believe: Loving my mom more means loving me more.

The role of the stepparent is often unclear, and nowhere is the uncertainty more apparent than when it comes to discipline. We all have rather firm ideas about how children should be raised. Yet, stepfamilies have a history of expectations. You cannot walk in one day and impose your own. At least initially, leave the task of discipline to the biological parent. Before you assume some of that responsibility, you must build credibility and rapport with your stepchildren and learn about their individual temperaments. You cannot simply assume that what worked for you or your biological children will work for them. And by staying away from the disciplinary role, your initial interactions with your stepchildren will be positive ones.

Disciplining is tough under any circumstances, but it is especially so when a child feels, "Who do you think you are, telling me what to do. You're not my real parent." Your new spouse may also be inclined to second-guess your efforts at discipline in any case. "They're my children. I'll tell them what they can and cannot do!" But just as in the biological family, parents must present a united front to their children. If your new wife overrules your decisions, she undercuts any potential respect her children may develop toward you. She also reinforces the psychological boundary that includes her and her children and excludes you.

Single parents often allow their children more latitude than we see in a two-parent household. This may be more latitude than you feel comfortable with. Parents are also much more tolerant of their own children's faults than the faults of other children.

You must talk with your spouse-to-be about both of your expectations of child behavior before you enter your new family. What will the rules, routines (e.g., sleeping, eating), and privileges (e.g., allowance) be? What are the responsibilities and chores of the children? What values do you wish to impart to the children? How are children allowed to express their feelings? What kinds of discipline tools will be used? At some point, you will become involved as disciplinarian. When should that be? (Ironically, avoiding any disciplining may be interpreted by stepchildren as, "You don't care.")

When both parents bring children with them to the new marriage, the circumstances obviously become fraught with even more opportunities for disagreement and conflict over discipline. Stepfamilies may come together at different points in life (e.g., one set of children may be preschoolers and another set teenagers), requiring different ways of regulating behavior. Therefore, parents may have to adjust their reflexive responses to their "new" children. And younger children, for example, will have to learn to cope with their jealousy of the greater leeway given to their older stepsiblings.

Hopefully, love will come. Your stepchildren will appreciate the fact that you are the adult who is willing to take on the daily responsibilities of parenting them. And just as importantly, your stepchildren will begin to understand that loving you does not preclude them from loving their "real dad."

"Who Do You Think You Are?"

Perhaps the most unnerving issue for stepchildren is *loyalty*. No matter whether the biological father is dead or divorced, a child will experience the remarriage of the mother as an act of disloyalty to him. How could she be happy, *even happier*, with another man? they condemningly wonder. How could she have forced my father out of our home and let this stranger take his place?

Not surprisingly then, a stepchild may feel displaced by you. His previous special relationship with his mother has been usurped. "Before, I had all of her love and attention. Now, I have to (at best) share her with you. How could she do this to me? Who does she really care about, anyway?" Inevitably, this child will repeatedly test his mother by putting his stepfather's interests against his own and forcing his mother to choose. Whose side are you on? he wants to know.

A stepchild idealizes his previous family and wishes for its reconstitution. A stepfather is an intruder, an obstacle who is, therefore, keeping the family from getting back together. At best, a stepchild will feel ambivalent toward you. He might like a new father so that he will, once again, have a "normal" family. But he also enjoyed having his mother to himself. And no matter how much your stepchildren may like you, they will be torn by their feelings of loyalty to their biological father. Even if you are a great stepdad (and everything their previous father was not), to acknowledge this would imply a rejection or derogation of their real father.

Ultimately, the stepchild fears you. He fears the loss of his routines. He fears the changes you will bring to his life. He fears the loss of another parent. He fears that his mother will no longer need him.

Competing with Ghosts

A child always prefers to be with his "real" parent. Children particularly idealize and long for a parent who has died. So in some sense a stepparent is always unwanted, whether replacing a parent who is alive or one who is dead. Sometimes that's hard for a stepfather to understand. "I know their real father. He was a complete jerk, a bully. He didn't care about anybody but himself." But that's not how he is being remembered from afar. (He also may *become* more generous in the present during his contacts with his children as he attempts to prove his love despite his absence.)

Never speak ill of your stepchild's father. Loyalty to the image of his father the child carries with him will only compel him to resent your remarks. Never strike a posture of, "I want to make up for what a lousy father you had." On the contrary, barring a situation of abuse, you should encourage your stepchild's relationship with his biological father. By doing so, you will quell your stepchild's fears and conflicts surrounding faithfulness.

Should you legally adopt your stepchildren? Legal adoption usually occurs when the biological parent has lost or avoids contact with his child for a protracted period of time. Even with this desertion, however, a biological parent must legally consent to the adoption of his minor child. Adoption may provide a stepchild with a greater sense of psychological and financial security about the relationship. But asking a child if he wishes to be adopted may also trigger traitorous feelings about his real father. And remember, adoption will not create instant love.

Stepsiblings

Children are jealous of the attention and love which their siblings receive from mommy and daddy. This competitiveness and rivalry is magnified among stepsiblings. From the outset, stepsiblings will be wary of one another. They will feel threatened and fear displacement. Do not expect love to predominate stepsibling relationships.

Integrating stepsiblings is particularly difficult when one or both sets had previously been part of a single-parent household for a protracted period. This time allowed for an especially intense bond to develop between the children and their solo parent. A mutually protective relationship may have ensued, thus creating the even greater likelihood of alliances and barriers between "opposing camps."

If financially and practically possible, a blended stepfamily should begin in a new home so that issues of territoriality do not immediately arise. Nevertheless, smooth stepfamily integration may take years as a new family identity takes shape. But stepparents working as a team can hasten that process. However, because stepsibling rivalries become intertwined with vulnerabilities caused by the loss of their previous family units and feelings of loyalty to the absent biological parents, professional assistance may be required.

A Father's Loyalties

Children always experience conflicts of loyalty between a stepparent and a biological parent. (Therefore, for example, never ask your biological child for permission to remarry.) Parents also experience conflicts of loyalty between their absent children and their stepchildren. If you are a noncustodial father, you will struggle with guilt as well. Guilt about spending more time with your stepchildren than your own children. Guilt about having less money for your real son and daughter because you are now supporting another family. Unfortunately, your stepchildren and new spouse will probably be jealously monitoring which family is favored, which family is getting more, thereby increasing the pressures you feel.

Your guilt about leaving your children may paralyze your

ability to bond with your stepchildren. Your guilt may cause you to defer to your children instead of your new wife. Your guilt will make it easy for your biological children to manipulate you, and you will be placed frequently in situations where you are effectively asked to choose between your real children and "her kids." While you remain mired in guilt, you may also continue to undeservedly blame yourself for any problems which your children develop. In turn, your attitude will reinforce your children's tendency to blame you as well, instead of taking responsibility for their behavior and their lives.

Ideally, if you and your ex have resolved your grievances, your children will be able to freely move back and forth between your respective households. (If she remains spiteful, she will probably continue to denigrate you, which may feed your children's anger and emotional withdrawal from your relationship.) When your children do visit, they must obey the rules of your home. Do not treat them as guests. If, for example, your stepchildren who are comparable in age to your own children have chores, your biological children should have responsibilities as well. If your biological children can have a room of their own where they can keep their toys, clothes, books, etc., they are less likely to feel like interlopers. Your stepchildren will also be less likely to feel resentful because their lives are being disrupted when a visit occurs.

Visitations are emotional roller coasters for everyone concerned. You always hope visits will be enjoyable and rewarding. You may fear your children will have become emotionally disconnected from you under the influence of your bitter ex or as a result of their own anger at feeling betrayed. After their fleeting stay, saying good-bye is heartbreaking, as it highlights the absence of a normal father-child relationship. Each visit makes it feel as if they have slipped away from you a little more. Each time you are reminded of what you have lost.

Your new spouse will be anxious to make your children's stay a pleasurable one. She may hope for some relationship as well. Unfortunately, many of her attempts will be rebuffed. Your biological children will be on the lookout for any changes in you or how you feel about them and how you feel about your "new" children. Their fears may make them defensive, and their defensiveness may cause them to be aloof and sullen. Your stepchildren will be acutely aware of your shift of attention and will compare the quality of your usual interactions with them against the quality of your interactions with your "real" children. When your "real" children leave, your stepchildren will wonder how much of your heart has gone with them and how much remains.

The Package Deal

Stepparents are catapulted into parenthood. While you were romancing your wife-to-be, you were understandably focused on her. Your prospective stepchildren were on the periphery. Furthermore, you could not have possibly fully anticipated what it would be like when all of you would be living together on a day-to-day basis.

If you did not have previous children of your own, you were completely unprepared for the mess, the noise level, the stubbornness, the insolence, the egocentrism, or the irrationality which children offer. And because these are not your own children, you will have even less patience for any of it.

Raising stepchildren brings its attendant marital tensions which you did not anticipate either. You were unprepared for the jealousy and feelings of intrusion of your stepchildren. ("Don't they understand I'm not going to take their mother away from them?") You were unprepared to bite your tongue and defer disciplinary responsibilities to your new wife. You were unprepared for the divided loyalties she would experience. You were unprepared for the fact that she would love her children more than she would love you.

In the atypical situation where your new, childless wife joins you and your biological children from a previous marriage, she, too, enters a novel circumstance for which she is unprepared. Despite her best intentions as a stepmom, she will resent the unanticipated demands. While prepared to love and care about her stepchildren, she will be unprepared for their ongoing rejection. She will resent the possessiveness her stepchildren show toward her husband, especially the bond between daughter and father. Her stepchildren will hate her intrusion into their lives and any of her attempts to discipline them. Before your new wife and you have had an opportunity to solidify your "oneness," loyalty conflicts will manifest themselves between you.

Your children may act as if they are conspiring to break up your new marriage. And on some conscious or unconscious level, their intention may be just that, as they put you in the continuous, untenable position of choosing between her and them.

"Dad, she's a loser."

"No, you're wrong."

(I knew he would choose her over me.)

While they may not expect it from their biological children, stepparents expect gratitude from their stepchildren. You may see yourself as having rescued them from economic and physical privations. "I'm giving all of this to them and they're not even mine," you say to yourself. "Here I am, taking care of them and I don't *have* to," you believe. And then you compare yourself to what you have heard about their biological father, and you feel particularly saintly.

And what do you get in return? Your stepchildren's anger—because who they desperately want is their real dad.

Money

Sometimes, it seems as though you just can't win. When you give money to your biological family, your new family resents you. When you bestow a gift on your new family, your biological family feels betrayed. While you are supporting two households, your new wife is angry at having inherited your previous obligations, and your ex-wife resents her continuing dependence on your paycheck. Any act of generosity on your part can stoke flames of jealousy in all other parties.

Money can become a powerful symbol of your love. (That's one of the reasons prenuptial agreements feel so hurtful.) Even if it is your money, your new wife will be angry if you offer expensive gifts or make major financial decisions regarding your biological family without consulting her. And even if you are not legally bound to support your stepchildren, you probably feel a sense of obligation to your new spouse, for you are reminded of the old adage: Love me, love my children. You may be further prodded to accept this responsibility by the likelihood that your wife's former spouse cut off his child support when she hooked up with you.

Money offers proof of your commitment. And everyone will be watching you to see where you stand.

Having Another Child

The decision to have a child with your new mate will cause insecurities in both your old and new families. For your new wife, your biological children, and your stepchildren, this new child provides an additional test of your loyalty. How does this choice effect and reflect your feelings about me? they all wonder.

Often, having a child with a new spouse strengthens the marital bond immeasurably. However, another child may also cause new financial pressures. And particularly when the husband is considerably older than the wife and has already raised children from a previous marriage, he may balk at the idea of reverting to the bottle-and-diaper stage again.

Before you decided to marry for the first time, you only had your feelings to sort out. While your ambivalence may have generated some agonizing moments, it was simple compared to the complexity of anticipating and considering the feelings of biological children, an ex-spouse, a new wife, and stepchildren. Before your first marriage, you talked with yourself about what the future might look like. Before you remarry, you must talk with your children and reassure them of your constancy; you must talk with your prospective wife about both of your expectations regarding her children, your children, her ex, your ex, and your relationships with all of them. Don't expect that "everything will work out as we become more comfortable with one another." On the contrary. It won't be smooth. And it won't be easy.

Stepparenting will present you with many challenges. It can also present you with rewards. The reward of helping apprehensive children overcome their anxieties and feelings of mistrust. The reward of helping children feel lovable again. The reward of giving unselfishly to your new family.

The Ongoing Process

> Do everything right, all the time, and the child will prosper. It's as simple as that, except for fate, luck, heredity, chance, and the astrological sign under which the child was born, his order of birth, his first encounter with evil, the girl who jilts him in spite of her excellent qualities, the war that is being fought when he is a young man, the drugs he may try once or too many times, the friends he makes, how he scores on tests, how well he endures kidding about his shortcomings, how ambitious he becomes, how far he falls behind, circumstantial evidence, ironic perspective, danger when it's least expected, difficulty in triumphing over circumstances, people with hidden agendas, and animals with rabies.
>
> ANN BEATTIE

While you may not have as much control as you would like in your work world, you can have the continuous satisfaction of ongoing involvement in the world of your family. As with most other aspects of life, you will reap what you sow. With regard to your children, you will get back what you put in, usually with interest. Your children have much love to give you, if only you will give them the opening.

We can love, encourage, and reassure our children, but we

can't always protect them from their inevitable stumbles. We wish we could guarantee their happiness, but of course, we can't. Remember that part of the growing-up process involves learning how to cope with disappointment. Remember that loving your children means believing in their abilities. Loving your children does *not* mean making their lives easy.

You can give your child the fertile conditions necessary for a close relationship. But the closeness of your relationship will also fluctuate with your child's needs for independence. Some parents experience this distancing as a rejection. But loving your child also means letting go and encouraging self-reliance.

Children take everything personally. Developmentally ego-centric, they are preoccupied with themselves and exaggerate their impact on the world around them. If you are unavailable, children are prone to believe it is because they are unlovable. Loving you comes naturally for them. Since they believe it should come naturally from you as well, they will find some reason to blame themselves if it is absent.

Most parenting books deal with only one side of the issue. They fail to fully appreciate the role which a good marriage can play in boosting the level of father-child interaction. If your marriage is a satisfying one, you will want to become more involved in family life. If your marriage is a cooperative one, you will be able to present a united front to your children and build the respect your children have for each of you. If your marriage is a loving one, you will provide a role model which your children will want to reach for when they grow up.

You must love yourself before you will be able to love your children. Loving yourself should not imply self-indulgence. When you are too self-involved, you will not think about what your children need from you. Loving yourself entails accepting yourself. You may never be the most involved father on earth. But hopefully, after reading this book, you will be a more involved father.

You will make mistakes. Fortunately, children are very resilient and will continue to want you and love you. Of course, no matter what you do, your children will not turn out perfectly, nor will they turn out exactly as you hope. But they will be special in their own way. Fill them up with love and not criticism. Give them the self-esteem they will need to meet life's challenges.

Why did you have children if not to be with them, if not to be close to them? Don't be a spectator at your child's development, be a participant. Don't simply get caught up in their whirlwind of activities. Make sure there are quiet moments to talk, to hear, to understand, to connect. Cherish each day with your children. They will be gone all too soon.

The time and energy you put into parenting will be rewarded through the generations. The parenting you received was probably due, in no small measure, to the parenting which your mother and/or father received. The kind of parent you are will influence the kind of parent your child will become. Give your grandchildren and great-grandchildren a head start.

If we love our children more, if we invest more in them, we will have more empathy for all children. If we see every soldier as someone's child, it will be more difficult to kill him. If we see all human beings as someone's son or daughter, it will be more difficult to hate them.

Fathering presents a continuous challenge of looking deep inside ourselves and understanding what we must restrain and what we must contribute to our child's development. We are not born fathers. We become fathers. And the process is an ongoing one.

When I have asked fathers, "What didn't you anticipate about being a parent?", perhaps the most common response has been, "Just how *difficult* it was going to be." Ultimately, as a parent, you will do the best you can. However, just make sure that you do not underestimate your abilities. And keep your gaze focused on what is really important in life. Love your children.

Then, love them a little more.